BELGIUM

TRAVEL GUIDE 2025

Your Complete Handbook to Experience
Bruges, Brussels, Antwerp & Ghent

WILLIAM SIDES

Copyright © 2025 William Sides. All rights reserved.

This book is protected under international copyright laws. No part of this publication may be reproduced, distributed, or transmitted in any form or by any means, including photocopying, recording, or other electronic or mechanical methods, without the prior written permission of the author or publisher, except in the case of brief quotations used in reviews or critical articles.

Disclaimer

The information in this book is provided for general guidance and informational purposes only. While every effort has been made to ensure the accuracy and reliability of the content, the author and publisher make no guarantees or warranties, expressed or implied, regarding the completeness, accuracy, or suitability of the information for any purpose.

Travel conditions, prices, and services may change over time, and readers are encouraged to verify details with relevant sources before making travel plans. The author and publisher are not responsible for any loss, injury, or inconvenience caused by the use of the information in this book.

This book is not affiliated with or endorsed by any official tourism board, government agency, or organization mentioned within. All trademarks, service marks, and product names mentioned are the property of their respective owners. By using this book, you agree to take full responsibility for your travel decisions and actions.

TABLE OF CONTENTS

MAP OF BELGIUM 8

INTRODUCTION 9

WHY VISIT BELGIUM? 13

CHAPTER 1 17

THE HISTORY OF BELGIUM 17

CHAPTER 2 23

PLANNING YOUR TRIP 23

    Best Times to Visit Belgium 23

    Packing Guidelines for Belgium's Weather 27

    Budgeting Tips for Your Adventure 31

    Travel Apps and Tools for Tourists 35

CHAPTER 3 39

GETTING TO AND AROUND BELGIUM.................. 39

Arrival Information: Airports, Trains, and Highways in Belgium... 39

Transportation Options: Trains, Trams, Buses, and Bikes 45

CHAPTER 4 49

ACCOMMODATION OPTIONS IN BELGIUM 49

Luxury Accommodations in Bruges, Brussels, Antwerp, and Ghent 49

Mid-Range Hotels and Boutique Stays in Bruges, Brussels, Antwerp, and Ghent 56

Budget-Friendly Hostels and Guesthouses in Bruges, Brussels, Antwerp, and Ghent 63

CHAPTER 5 70

DINING IN BELGIUM 70

Famous Belgian Foods: Waffles, Chocolate, Fries, and More 70

Restaurants by Price Range 73

Street Food Recommendations and Food Markets 74

Best Breweries and Trappist Beers 75

CHAPTER 6 78

TOP TOURIST ATTRACTIONS IN BELGIUM 78

Bruges: Canals, Belfry, and the Markt......................... 78

Brussels: Grand Place, Atomium, and European Parliament 82

Antwerp: Cathedral of Our Lady, Rubens House, and Diamond District.. 87

Ghent: Gravensteen Castle, St. Bavo's Cathedral, and the Graslei 92

Hidden Gems and Lesser-Known Attractions in Belgium 100

CHAPTER 7 108

CULTURAL EXPERIENCES IN BELGIUM 108

Art and Architecture: Flemish Masters and Art Nouveau 108

Festivals and Events: Carnival, Ommegang, and More 115

Belgian Etiquette and Customs 121

Expected Behavior in Public Spaces........................... 124

Language Tips: Dutch, French, and English............... 126

CHAPTER 8 132

ADVENTURE AND OUTDOOR ACTIVITIES 132

Hiking and Nature Walks... 132

Water-Based Activities 134

Adventure Sports 136

Relaxed Outdoor Experiences...................................... 137

CHAPTER 9 140

NIGHTLIFE IN BELGIUM 140

Popular Venues 140

Best Neighborhoods for Nightlife Activities 143

CHAPTER 10 146

SHOPPING IN BELGIUM 146

What to Buy in Belgium 146

Where to Shop in Belgium... 148

CHAPTER 11 152

SAFETY AND EMERGENCY INFORMATION 152

    Safety Tips for Crowded Areas 152

    Emergency Contact Information 154

CHAPTER 12 158

DAY TRIP RECOMMENDATIONS 158

    Nearby Destinations 158

    Transportation Options for Day Trips 161

    Seasonal Considerations 162

CHAPTER 13 164

LANGUAGE AND COMMUNICATION 164

    Language Overview 164

    Common Phrases and Greetings 165

    Using English in Belgium 167

CHAPTER 14 170

ITINERARIES FOR EVERY TRAVELER 170

Itineraries for Solo Travelers 170

Itineraries for Couples 177

Itineraries for Families 183

> 3-Day Family Itinerary: A Short and Sweet Adventure 183
>
> 7-Day Family Itinerary: A Week of Fun and Exploration 186
>
> 14-Day Family Itinerary: A Comprehensive Belgian Adventure 188

CONCLUSION 190

MAP OF BELGIUM

SCAN THIS QR CODE
1. Open your phone's camera or QR code scanner app.
2. Point your camera at the QR code.
3. Wait for the QR code to be detected.
4. Tap the notification or link that appears.
5. Follow the link or instructions provided.

INTRODUCTION

Belgium is a country that feels like it was plucked straight out of a storybook. With its cobblestone streets, medieval architecture, and charming canals, it offers a timeless beauty that captivates every traveler who sets foot on its soil. As you explore this guide, you'll discover a land where history, culture, and modernity blend seamlessly, creating a destination that is as diverse as it is enchanting. Belgium is not just a place you visit; it's a place you experience, with all your senses coming alive to its sights, sounds, and flavors.

Imagine strolling through the heart of Bruges, where the air is filled with the aroma of freshly baked waffles, and the sound of horse-drawn carriages echoes through the narrow streets. The city's canals, often called the "Venice of the North," reflect the spires of Gothic churches and the colorful facades of centuries-old buildings. In Brussels, the capital, you'll find a city that is both the beating heart of Europe and a treasure trove of art, history, and culture. From the grandeur of the Grand Place to the quirky charm of the Manneken Pis, Brussels is a city that surprises and delights at every turn.

Antwerp, on the other hand, is a city of contrasts. Known as the diamond capital of the world, it dazzles with its opulent jewelry stores and vibrant fashion scene. But it's also a city steeped in history, where you can walk in the footsteps of

Flemish masters like Rubens and admire their works in stunning cathedrals and museums. And then there's Ghent, a city that feels like a hidden gem waiting to be discovered. With its medieval castles, bustling markets, and lively student culture, Ghent offers a perfect mix of old-world charm and youthful energy.

Belgium is a country that knows how to celebrate life. Its festivals, from the colorful Carnival of Binche to the flower-filled spectacle of the Ghent Floralies, are a testament to its vibrant culture and love for tradition. And then there's the food—oh, the food! Belgium is a paradise for food lovers, with its world-famous chocolates, golden fries, and an endless variety of beers brewed by monks in centuries-old abbeys. Every meal here is an experience, a chance to savor the rich flavors and culinary heritage of this small but mighty country.

But Belgium is not just about its cities and cuisine. It's a country of breathtaking landscapes, from the rolling hills of the Ardennes to the sandy beaches of the North Sea coast. Whether you're hiking through lush forests, cycling along scenic routes, or simply enjoying a quiet moment in a picturesque village, Belgium's natural beauty is sure to leave you in awe.

As you journey through this guide, you'll find everything you need to plan your perfect trip to Belgium. From practical tips on transportation and accommodations to detailed insights into the best attractions and hidden gems, this guide is your ultimate companion.

WHY VISIT BELGIUM?

Belgium is a destination that feels like it was designed to enchant every kind of traveler. Whether you're drawn to history, art, food, or simply the joy of discovering a place that feels both timeless and vibrant, Belgium has something extraordinary to offer. It's a country where every corner tells a story, every meal is a celebration, and every experience leaves you with memories to treasure.

Picture yourself wandering through medieval streets lined with centuries-old buildings, their facades adorned with intricate details that whisper tales of the past. In Belgium, history isn't confined to museums—it's alive in the cobblestone squares, the towering cathedrals, and the quiet canals that reflect the beauty of the cities around them. You can feel the weight of time as you stand in the shadow of a Gothic church or explore a castle that has stood for hundreds of years. Belgium's rich history is woven into its very fabric, and as you explore, you'll find yourself stepping into a world where the past and present coexist in perfect harmony.

But Belgium isn't just about looking back—it's a country that celebrates the here and now with a vibrant culture that's impossible to resist. From the bustling markets filled with the aroma of fresh produce and flowers to the lively festivals that light up the streets with music and color, Belgium is a place where life is lived to the fullest. The people here are warm and welcoming, always ready to share their love for their country with a smile and a story. Whether you're sipping a Trappist beer in a cozy pub or chatting with a chocolatier about their craft, you'll feel a genuine connection to the heart of Belgium.

And then there's the food. Belgium is a paradise for food lovers, a place where every bite is a revelation. Imagine savoring a plate of golden, crispy fries served with a dollop of creamy mayonnaise, or indulging in a piece of chocolate so rich and smooth it feels like it's melting into your soul. From hearty stews to delicate pastries, Belgium's culinary scene is as diverse as it is delicious. And let's not forget the beer—Belgium is home to some of the finest brews in the world, each one crafted with care and tradition. Whether you're a foodie or just someone who appreciates a good meal, Belgium will leave your taste buds dancing with delight.

For those who love art and architecture, Belgium is a treasure trove of inspiration. The works of Flemish masters like Rubens and Van Eyck adorn the walls of grand museums and churches, while the Art Nouveau buildings of Brussels showcase a more modern kind of beauty. Everywhere you look, there's something to admire, from the intricate lacework of a medieval guildhall to the bold lines of a contemporary sculpture. Belgium is a place where creativity thrives, and as you explore, you'll find yourself constantly amazed by the artistry that surrounds you.

Nature lovers will also find plenty to love in Belgium. The rolling hills of the Ardennes, the sandy beaches of the North Sea coast, and the tranquil beauty of the countryside offer a peaceful escape from the hustle and bustle of city life. Whether you're hiking through a forest, cycling along a scenic route, or simply enjoying a quiet moment by a river, Belgium's natural landscapes are a reminder of the simple joys of being outdoors.

And when it comes to entertainment, Belgium knows how to put on a show. From the lively nightlife of Antwerp to the charming cafes of Bruges, there's always something happening, always a new experience waiting to be had. Whether you're dancing the night away, enjoying a live concert, or simply soaking up the atmosphere of a bustling square, you'll find that Belgium has a way of making every moment feel special.

Belgium is a country that invites you to slow down, to savor the little things, and to immerse yourself in its charm. It's a place where you can lose yourself in the beauty of a medieval city, find inspiration in a masterpiece, and connect with a culture that's as rich and diverse as its history.

CHAPTER 1
THE HISTORY OF BELGIUM

Belgium's history is a story of transformation, resilience, and cultural brilliance, spanning centuries of remarkable events and achievements. As you walk through its cities and countryside, you'll find that every corner of Belgium tells a tale, from its medieval roots to its modern role as a hub of European unity. This small but influential country has been at the crossroads of European history, shaped by its strategic location, its artistic and intellectual contributions, and its enduring spirit.

In the medieval period, Belgium was not yet a unified nation but a collection of prosperous territories that formed part of the Low Countries. These lands, including Flanders, Brabant, and Hainaut, were among the most economically and culturally advanced regions in Europe. The cities of Bruges, Ghent, and Antwerp became thriving centers of trade, thanks to their strategic locations along rivers and trade routes. Bruges, in particular, was a hub of the Hanseatic League, a powerful network of trading cities that dominated commerce in northern Europe. Its canals, which still charm visitors today, were once bustling with ships carrying wool, spices, and other valuable goods. The wealth generated by this trade transformed these cities into cultural and architectural marvels, where grand town halls, ornate guildhalls, and towering cathedrals were built to showcase their prosperity.

The medieval period also saw the rise of the Flemish Masters, a group of extraordinary artists who revolutionized European art. Jan van Eyck, often regarded as the father of oil painting, brought an unprecedented level of detail and realism to his works. His masterpiece, the *Ghent Altarpiece*, is a stunning example of his skill, with its intricate depictions of religious figures and landscapes. Pieter Bruegel the Elder, another towering figure, captured the spirit of the 16th century with his vivid and often humorous depictions of peasant life, festivals, and landscapes. His works, such as *The Harvesters* and *The Peasant Wedding*, offer a glimpse into the daily lives of ordinary people, blending realism with a deep sense of humanity. Peter Paul Rubens, a master of the Baroque era, brought drama, emotion, and grandeur to his paintings, which adorned churches, palaces, and galleries across Europe. These artists not only shaped the course of European art but also cemented Belgium's reputation as a land of creativity and innovation.

As the medieval period gave way to the Renaissance and beyond, Belgium became a key player in European politics and culture. In the 15th century, the region came under the rule of the Dukes of Burgundy, who transformed the Low Countries into a cultural and economic powerhouse. The Burgundian court was one of the most sophisticated in Europe, attracting artists, musicians, and scholars from far and wide. This period saw the construction of many of the stunning buildings that still grace Belgium's cities today, from the Gothic spires of town halls to the intricate facades of guildhalls. The Burgundian influence also extended to the arts, with the Flemish Masters continuing to produce works of unparalleled beauty and innovation.

In the 16th century, Belgium became part of the vast Habsburg Empire, first under Spanish rule and later under Austrian control. This was a time of great upheaval, as the Protestant Reformation swept through Europe, challenging the authority of the Catholic Church. The Low Countries became a battleground for religious and political conflicts, with Belgium remaining largely Catholic while its northern neighbor, the Netherlands, embraced Protestantism. Despite these challenges, Belgium continued to thrive as a center of art and culture, with its cities remaining vibrant and cosmopolitan.

The 19th century marked a turning point in Belgium's history. In 1830, the country declared its independence from the Netherlands, establishing itself as a constitutional monarchy. This was a time of great change, as Belgium embraced the Industrial Revolution and became a leader in industries such as textiles, steel, and coal. The country's railways, among the most advanced in the world, connected its cities and fueled its economic growth. At the same time, Belgium's cultural scene flourished, with writers, musicians, and artists making their mark on the world stage.

Belgium's role in European history is perhaps most poignant in the context of the two World Wars. During World War I, the country was the site of some of the most brutal battles, including the infamous trench warfare of Flanders Fields. The poppies that grew on these battlefields became a symbol of remembrance, and today, the region is dotted with cemeteries and memorials that honor the millions who lost their lives. In World War II, Belgium was again occupied, and its cities and towns bore the scars of conflict. Yet, through it all, the Belgian people showed incredible resilience, rebuilding their country and looking to the future with hope.

In the post-war era, Belgium emerged as a symbol of unity and cooperation. As one of the founding members of the European Union, it has played a central role in shaping the future of Europe. Brussels, the capital, is now home to the EU's headquarters, as well as NATO, making it a hub of international diplomacy. This spirit of collaboration is deeply rooted in Belgium's history, a testament to its ability to bring people together and find common ground.

Today, Belgium's history is not just something to be studied—it's something to be experienced. It's in the medieval streets of Bruges, where the past feels just a step away. It's in the grand squares of Brussels, where Gothic and Baroque architecture stand side by side. It's in the art that graces its museums, the traditions that fill its festivals, and the stories that echo through its landscapes. Belgium's past is a rich and complex tapestry, one that continues to shape its present and inspire its future.

As you explore Belgium, you'll find that its history is more than just dates and events—it's a living, breathing part of the country's identity. It's a story of resilience, creativity, and connection, one that invites you to step back in time and discover the moments that made Belgium what it is today.

CHAPTER 2
PLANNING YOUR TRIP

Best Times to Visit Belgium

Belgium is a country that offers something special no matter when you visit. Each season brings its own unique charm, transforming the landscapes, cities, and experiences in ways that make every trip memorable. Whether you're drawn to the blooming beauty of spring, the lively energy of summer, the golden hues of autumn, or the cozy magic of winter, Belgium has a way of captivating you with its ever-changing character. Understanding the seasons and what they bring can help you plan the perfect trip, tailored to your preferences and interests.

Spring in Belgium is a time of renewal and color. From March to May, the country awakens from its winter slumber, and the landscapes burst into life with vibrant flowers and lush greenery. The weather is mild, with temperatures ranging from 8°C to 15°C (46°F to 59°F), making it ideal for exploring the countryside or strolling through the cobblestone streets of cities like Bruges and Ghent. This is also the season when Belgium's famous tulip fields and gardens come into full bloom, creating breathtaking displays of color. The Royal Greenhouses of Laeken, near Brussels, open their doors to the public for a few weeks in spring, offering a rare chance to see their stunning collection of exotic plants and flowers. Spring is also a time for festivals, such as the Floralia flower show and the lively Easter markets, which add a festive touch to the season.

As summer arrives, Belgium comes alive with energy and excitement. From June to August, the days are long and warm, with temperatures averaging between 18°C and 25°C (64°F to 77°F). This is the perfect time to enjoy outdoor activities, whether it's cycling along scenic routes, relaxing on the sandy beaches of the North Sea coast, or taking a boat ride through the canals of Bruges. Belgium's cities are buzzing with life, as locals and visitors alike gather in open-air cafes, parks, and squares to soak up the sunshine. Summer is also the season of festivals, and Belgium is famous for its vibrant celebrations. The Tomorrowland music festival, one of the largest electronic dance music events in the world, draws thousands of visitors to Boom, while the Gentse Feesten in Ghent offers ten days of music, theater, and street performances. The Brussels Summer Festival and the Rock Werchter music festival are also highlights of the season, showcasing Belgium's love for music and culture. If you're a fan of beer, summer is the perfect time to visit one of Belgium's many breweries or beer gardens, where you can sample refreshing Trappist ales and other local brews.

Autumn in Belgium is a season of golden beauty and quiet charm. From September to November, the weather begins to cool, with temperatures ranging from 10°C to 18°C (50°F to 64°F), and the landscapes are painted in shades of red, orange, and yellow. This is a wonderful time to explore Belgium's forests and countryside, where the changing leaves create a picturesque backdrop for hiking and cycling. The Ardennes region, in particular, is stunning in autumn, with its rolling hills and dense woodlands offering a peaceful escape from the cities. In the towns and cities, the autumn months bring a sense of coziness, as cafes and restaurants begin to serve hearty seasonal dishes like stews and soups. Autumn is also a time for harvest festivals and food events, such as the Brussels Beer Weekend and the Fête de la Gastronomie, which celebrate Belgium's culinary heritage. The quieter atmosphere of autumn makes it an ideal time for those who prefer a more relaxed and intimate travel experience, with fewer crowds and a slower pace.

Winter in Belgium is a season of warmth and wonder, despite the chilly weather. From December to February, temperatures typically range from 0°C to 7°C (32°F to 45°F), and the cities take on a magical quality as they are adorned with twinkling lights and festive decorations. The Christmas markets are a highlight of the season, with Brussels, Bruges, and Ghent hosting some of the most enchanting markets in Europe. Here, you can sip on mulled wine, sample traditional treats like waffles and speculoos cookies, and shop for handmade gifts and ornaments. Winter is also a time for ice skating, with rinks set up in city squares, and for enjoying the cozy ambiance of Belgium's cafes and pubs, where you can warm up with a hot chocolate or a rich Belgian beer. For those who enjoy history and culture, winter is a great time to visit Belgium's museums and galleries, which are less crowded during this season. The Carnival of Binche, held in February, is another winter highlight, with its colorful parades and unique traditions earning it a place on UNESCO's list of Intangible Cultural Heritage.

No matter when you choose to visit, Belgium offers a wealth of experiences that reflect the character of each season. Spring brings renewal and color, summer offers energy and celebration, autumn provides tranquility and warmth, and winter delivers magic and festivity. Each season has its own rhythm, its own beauty, and its own way of making you fall in love with this remarkable country. By understanding what each time of year has to offer, you can plan a trip that matches your interests and ensures that your time in Belgium is as unforgettable as the country itself.

Packing Guidelines for Belgium's Weather

Packing for a trip to Belgium requires a bit of planning, as the country's weather can be unpredictable and varies significantly depending on the season. Whether you're visiting during the crisp days of spring, the warm and lively summer, the golden hues of autumn, or the chilly magic of winter, being prepared with the right clothing and essentials will ensure your trip is comfortable and enjoyable. Belgium's charm lies in its diversity of experiences, from exploring medieval cities to hiking in the Ardennes, so packing versatile and practical items is key.

If you're visiting Belgium in the spring, you'll want to be ready for mild but changeable weather. Temperatures typically range from 8°C to 15°C (46°F to 59°F), and while the days can be pleasantly warm, sudden rain showers are common. Lightweight, breathable clothing is ideal for layering, as it allows you to adjust to the fluctuating temperatures. A waterproof jacket or a compact umbrella is a must, as spring showers can catch you off guard while you're strolling through the cobblestone streets of Bruges or admiring the tulip fields. Comfortable walking shoes are essential, as you'll likely spend a lot of time exploring on foot. If you plan to visit gardens or parks, such as the Royal Greenhouses of Laeken, consider packing a pair of sturdy yet stylish shoes that can handle grassy or uneven terrain.

Summer in Belgium is warm and vibrant, with temperatures ranging from 18°C to 25°C (64°F to 77°F). This is the season for light, breathable fabrics like cotton and linen, which will keep you cool as you explore bustling markets, enjoy outdoor festivals, or relax at a café in the Grand Place. A wide-brimmed hat or a cap, along with sunglasses, will protect you from the sun during long days outdoors. While summer is generally dry, occasional rain showers can still occur, so a lightweight rain jacket or a travel umbrella is a good idea. Comfortable sandals or sneakers are perfect for walking around cities like Brussels and Antwerp, but if you're planning to cycle along scenic routes or hike in the countryside, pack a pair of sturdy athletic shoes. For evenings, when temperatures can drop slightly, a light sweater or cardigan will keep you comfortable. If you're attending a festival like Tomorrowland or the Gentse Feesten, consider bringing a small backpack or crossbody bag to carry essentials like water, sunscreen, and a portable phone charger.

Autumn in Belgium is a season of cozy charm, with temperatures cooling to between 10°C and 18°C (50°F to

64°F). The weather can be unpredictable, with sunny days giving way to rain and cooler evenings. Layering is your best friend during this time of year. Pack long-sleeved shirts, sweaters, and a medium-weight jacket to stay warm and comfortable. A scarf is a versatile accessory that can add warmth and style, especially if you're visiting picturesque towns like Ghent or Leuven, where the autumn colors create a stunning backdrop. Waterproof footwear is a smart choice, as the streets can become slippery with rain or fallen leaves. If you're planning to explore the Ardennes or other natural areas, bring hiking boots or sturdy shoes that can handle muddy trails. Autumn is also a great time to enjoy Belgium's culinary delights, so consider packing slightly dressier outfits for dining at cozy restaurants or attending food festivals like the Brussels Beer Weekend.

Winter in Belgium is cold but magical, with temperatures ranging from 0°C to 7°C (32°F to 45°F). To stay warm while exploring Christmas markets or admiring the festive lights in cities like Bruges and Brussels, pack a heavy coat, gloves, a hat, and a scarf. Thermal layers are a great addition, especially if you're planning to spend extended periods outdoors. Waterproof boots with good traction are essential for navigating icy or wet streets, and thick socks will keep your feet warm and comfortable. If you're visiting during the Carnival of Binche or other winter events, consider bringing a small backpack to carry extra layers or snacks. For indoor activities, such as visiting museums or enjoying a hot chocolate in a cozy café, pack comfortable yet stylish clothing that can be easily layered.

No matter the season, there are a few essentials that will make your trip to Belgium more enjoyable. A compact travel umbrella or a lightweight rain jacket is always a good idea, as rain can occur at any time of year. A reusable water bottle will keep you hydrated as you explore, and a daypack or crossbody bag is perfect for carrying your essentials while keeping your hands free. If you're planning to visit multiple cities, pack versatile clothing that can be mixed and matched to save space in your luggage. Don't forget a universal power adapter for charging your devices, as Belgium uses Type C and Type E outlets. Finally, a small first-aid kit with items like band-aids, pain relievers, and any personal medications will ensure you're prepared for minor inconveniences.

By packing thoughtfully and considering the season, you'll be ready to enjoy everything Belgium has to offer, from its historic cities to its stunning natural landscapes. With the right clothing and essentials, you can focus on creating unforgettable memories in this beautiful and welcoming country.

Budgeting Tips for Your Adventure

Traveling to Belgium can be an unforgettable experience, and with a little planning, you can enjoy everything this beautiful country has to offer without breaking the bank. Whether you're a budget-conscious traveler or looking to splurge on a few luxuries, understanding the typical costs and making smart choices can help you make the most of your trip. Belgium offers a range of options for accommodation, food, transportation, and attractions, so you can tailor your experience to suit your budget while still enjoying the country's rich culture, history, and charm.

When it comes to accommodation, Belgium has something for everyone, from budget-friendly hostels to luxurious boutique hotels. If you're traveling on a tight budget, you can find hostels or budget hotels in major cities like Brussels, Bruges, and Antwerp, with prices starting at around €25 to €40 per night for a dorm bed or a basic private room. Mid-range travelers can expect to pay between €80 and €150 per night for a comfortable hotel or guesthouse, often with amenities like free breakfast or Wi-Fi. For those seeking a more upscale experience, boutique hotels and luxury accommodations can range from €200 to €400 per night, offering elegant rooms, fine dining, and prime locations in historic city centers. Booking your stay in advance, especially during peak travel seasons, can help you secure better rates. If you're open to alternative options, consider renting an apartment or staying in a bed-and-breakfast, which can provide a more local and personalized experience.

Food is another area where Belgium caters to all budgets, and you'll find plenty of delicious options no matter how much you're willing to spend. For a quick and affordable meal, you can enjoy Belgium's famous fries, waffles, or a hearty sandwich from a street vendor or casual eatery for around €5 to €10. Local brasseries and cafes offer more substantial meals, such as stews, mussels, or pasta, with prices typically ranging from €15 to €25 per dish. If you're dining at a mid-range restaurant, expect to spend around €30 to €50 per person for a three-course meal, excluding drinks. For a fine dining experience, Belgium's Michelin-starred restaurants and gourmet establishments can cost upwards of €100 per person, but the quality and creativity of the cuisine make it a worthwhile splurge. To save money on food, consider visiting local markets, where you can pick up fresh produce, cheese, and bread for a picnic, or look for lunch specials and set menus, which often provide excellent value.

Transportation in Belgium is efficient and affordable, making it easy to explore the country without spending a fortune. The train network is extensive and connects major cities like Brussels, Bruges, Ghent, and Antwerp, with ticket prices ranging from €10 to €20 for a one-way journey between cities. If you plan to travel frequently by train, consider purchasing a rail pass, such as the Belgian Rail Pass, which allows you to take ten journeys for a fixed price, saving you money on individual tickets. Public transportation within cities is also convenient and budget-friendly, with trams, buses, and metro systems offering single tickets for around €2.50 to €3. Multi-day passes are available and can be a cost-effective option if you're staying in one city for several days. For shorter distances, walking or renting a bike is a great way to save money while enjoying the sights at your own pace. Taxis and ride-sharing services are available but can be expensive, so they're best reserved for late-night trips or when public transportation isn't an option.

Belgium's attractions and activities offer a mix of free and paid options, allowing you to experience the country's rich culture and history without overspending. Many of Belgium's most iconic landmarks, such as the Grand Place in Brussels, the canals of Bruges, and the historic squares of Ghent, can be enjoyed for free. Museums and galleries typically charge admission fees ranging from €8 to €15, but many offer free entry on specific days or discounted rates for students, seniors, and families. If you're planning to visit multiple attractions, look into city passes, such as the Brussels Card or the Antwerp City Card, which provide free or discounted entry to museums, public transportation, and other perks. Outdoor activities, such as hiking in the Ardennes or exploring the North Sea coast, are also budget-friendly options that showcase Belgium's natural beauty.

To stretch your budget further, there are several practical tips you can follow. Traveling during the off-season, from November to March, can help you save on flights and accommodation while avoiding the crowds. Booking train tickets and accommodations in advance often secures better rates, and using public transportation instead of taxis can significantly reduce your expenses. Dining at local eateries or opting for lunch specials can help you enjoy Belgium's culinary delights without overspending, and taking advantage of free walking tours is a great way to learn about the country's history and culture while keeping costs low. If you're a student or under 26, be sure to carry your ID, as many attractions and transportation services offer discounts for young travelers.

By planning thoughtfully and making smart choices, you can enjoy all that Belgium has to offer without worrying about your budget. Whether you're savoring a waffle in a bustling square, marveling at a masterpiece in a museum, or wandering through a medieval town, you'll find that Belgium's charm and beauty are accessible to travelers of all budgets. With a little preparation, you can create unforgettable memories while keeping your expenses under control, ensuring that your trip to Belgium is as enjoyable as it is affordable.

Travel Apps and Tools for Tourists

Traveling in Belgium becomes even more enjoyable and stress-free when you have the right apps and tools at your fingertips. With just a few downloads, you can navigate the country's cities with ease, discover hidden gems, and make the most of your time exploring everything Belgium has to offer. Whether you're planning your itinerary, finding the best places to eat, or figuring out how to get from one city to another, these apps can simplify your trip and help you feel more confident as you explore.

For navigation, Google Maps is an indispensable tool that will guide you through Belgium's winding streets, historic squares, and scenic countryside. It's perfect for finding your way around cities like Brussels, Bruges, and Antwerp, whether you're walking, driving, or using public transportation. The app provides real-time directions and updates, helping you avoid delays and find the quickest routes. One of its most useful features is the ability to download maps for offline use, which is especially handy if you're exploring areas with limited internet access. With Google Maps, you can also search for nearby attractions, restaurants, and shops, making it a one-stop solution for getting around and discovering new places.

When it comes to public transportation, the SNCB/NMBS app is a must-have for navigating Belgium's extensive train network. This app allows you to check train schedules, plan your journeys, and purchase tickets directly from your phone. It provides real-time updates on train arrivals and departures, so you'll always know if there are any delays or changes to your route. The app is user-friendly and available in multiple languages, making it accessible for international travelers. If you're planning to use trams, buses, or metro services within cities, the De Lijn app (for Flanders) and the TEC app (for Wallonia) are equally helpful. These apps provide detailed information on routes, schedules, and ticket options, ensuring that you can move around Belgium's cities with ease.

For dining and discovering the best local cuisine, the Yelp and TripAdvisor apps are excellent resources. These platforms allow you to browse reviews and recommendations for restaurants, cafes, and bars across Belgium. Whether you're looking for a cozy spot to enjoy traditional Belgian waffles or a Michelin-starred restaurant for a special evening, these apps can help you find exactly what you're craving. They also include photos, menus, and contact information, making it easy to decide where to eat and make reservations if needed. If you're in the mood for something spontaneous, these apps can also help you find highly rated eateries nearby, ensuring that you never miss out on Belgium's incredible food scene.

For ride-sharing and taxis, Uber is available in major cities like Brussels and Antwerp, offering a convenient and reliable way to get around. The app allows you to book rides quickly, track your driver's location, and pay directly through the platform, eliminating the need for cash. If you prefer traditional taxis, the Taxi.eu app is a great alternative, connecting you with licensed taxi services across Belgium. Both apps provide estimated fares and travel times, so you can plan your journeys with confidence.

To stay informed about local events and activities, the Visit Belgium app is a fantastic tool. This app is designed specifically for tourists and provides up-to-date information on festivals, exhibitions, concerts, and other events happening across the country. It also includes recommendations for attractions, guided tours, and cultural experiences, helping you make the most of your time in Belgium. The app's user-friendly interface and curated content make it easy to find activities that match your interests, whether you're a history buff, a foodie, or an art lover.

For language support, Google Translate is an invaluable companion, especially if you're traveling to areas where Dutch or French is predominantly spoken. The app allows you to translate text, speech, and even images, such as menus or signs, in real time. Its offline mode ensures that you can use it even without an internet connection, making it a reliable tool for overcoming language barriers and communicating with locals.

If you're looking for a way to save money on attractions and transportation, the City Cards apps for cities like Brussels, Antwerp, and Ghent are worth downloading. These apps provide information on city passes that offer free or discounted entry to museums, public transportation, and other perks. They also include maps and itineraries, helping you plan your days efficiently and get the most value out of your trip.

CHAPTER 3

GETTING TO AND AROUND BELGIUM

Arrival Information: Airports, Trains, and Highways in Belgium

Belgium is one of Europe's most accessible countries, with excellent connections by air, train, and road. Whether you're flying in, arriving by train, or driving, getting to Belgium is straightforward and convenient. Here's everything you need to know about arriving in Belgium and starting your journey smoothly.

Airports in Belgium

Belgium has several airports, but the main international gateway is **Brussels Airport (Zaventem)**. Located just 12 kilometers (7.5 miles) from the city center, it's well-connected to major cities around the world.

- **Brussels Airport (BRU)**: This is the largest and busiest airport in Belgium. It offers direct flights to and from cities across Europe, North America, Asia, and beyond. Once you land, you can easily reach the city center by train (20 minutes, around €9), bus, or taxi (approximately €45).

- **Brussels South Charleroi Airport (CRL)**: Located about 60 kilometers (37 miles) from Brussels, this airport is popular with budget airlines like Ryanair and Wizz Air. Shuttle buses run frequently between the airport and Brussels, with a travel time of about 1 hour (€17 one way).

- **Antwerp International Airport (ANR)**: A smaller airport mainly serving European destinations. It's just 5 kilometers (3 miles) from Antwerp's city center, making it a convenient option for travelers heading to this vibrant city.

- **Liège Airport (LGG)**: Located in eastern Belgium, this airport is smaller and primarily handles cargo flights, but it also offers some passenger services to select destinations.

Tips for Air Travelers:

- Book airport transfers or train tickets in advance to save time and money.

- Brussels Airport has excellent facilities, including luggage storage, currency exchange, and a wide range of shops and restaurants.

Trains in Belgium

Belgium's train network is one of the best in Europe, making it an ideal way to arrive and travel within the country. The **National Railway Company of Belgium (SNCB)** operates domestic and international trains, ensuring smooth connections to neighboring countries.

- **International Trains**:

    o **Eurostar**: Connects London to Brussels in just 2 hours via the Channel Tunnel.

    o **Thalys**: High-speed trains link Brussels with Paris (1.5 hours), Amsterdam (1.5 hours), and Cologne (2 hours).

    o **ICE (InterCity Express)**: Connects Brussels with German cities like Frankfurt and Düsseldorf.

    o **TGV**: High-speed trains to and from France, including Lyon and Marseille.

- **Domestic Trains**: Belgium's cities are well-connected by frequent and affordable trains. For example, you can travel from Brussels to Bruges in just 1 hour (€15.80 one way) or from Brussels to Antwerp in 40 minutes (€9.90 one way).

Major Train Stations

- **Brussels-Midi (Bruxelles-Midi/Brussel-Zuid)**: The main hub for international and domestic trains.

- **Antwerp-Central**: Known as one of the most beautiful train stations in the world.

- **Ghent-St. Pieters**: The main station for travelers heading to Ghent.

- **Bruges Station**: A short walk or bus ride from the historic city center.

Tips for Train Travelers:

- Book international train tickets in advance for the best prices.

- Domestic train tickets can be purchased on the day of travel, but check for discounts like weekend or youth passes.

- Use the **SNCB app** for real-time schedules and ticket purchases.

Highways and Driving in Belgium

Belgium's road network is extensive and well-maintained, making it easy to drive into the country from neighboring nations like France, Germany, the Netherlands, and Luxembourg.

- **Highways**: Belgium's highways are toll-free and well-lit, even at night. Major routes include:
    - **E40**: Connects Brussels to Bruges, Ghent, and the Belgian coast.
    - **E19**: Links Brussels with Antwerp and continues to the Netherlands.
    - **E411**: Runs from Brussels to Luxembourg.
- **Border Crossings**: There are no border checks between Belgium and other Schengen Area countries, so you can drive in freely.
- **Car Rentals**: Renting a car is a great option if you plan to explore rural areas like the Ardennes or smaller towns. Major rental companies like Hertz, Avis, and Europcar operate in Belgium's airports and cities.

Driving Tips:

- Drive on the right-hand side of the road.
- Speed limits: 120 km/h (75 mph) on highways, 90 km/h (56 mph) on rural roads, and 50 km/h (31 mph) in cities.
- Parking in city centers can be limited and expensive, so consider using park-and-ride facilities.

Which Option is Best for You?

- **Flying**: Ideal for international travelers arriving from outside Europe. Brussels Airport is the most convenient entry point.

- **Trains**: Perfect for those traveling from nearby European countries or exploring multiple cities within Belgium.

- **Driving**: Best for travelers who want to explore off-the-beaten-path destinations or enjoy the flexibility of a road trip.

Transportation Options: Trains, Trams, Buses, and Bikes

Getting around Belgium is a breeze, thanks to its well-connected and efficient transportation network. Whether you're exploring the bustling streets of Brussels, the charming canals of Bruges, or the historic squares of Ghent, Belgium offers a variety of transportation options to suit every traveler's needs. From subways and buses to taxis and car rentals, understanding how to navigate the country will help you make the most of your trip while saving time and effort.

Belgium's subway system, known as the metro, is primarily found in Brussels, the capital city. It's an excellent way to get around quickly and efficiently, especially if you're visiting popular attractions like the Grand Place, Atomium, or the European Parliament. The metro is clean, reliable, and easy to use, with four main lines that connect key areas of the city. Tickets can be purchased at vending machines in metro stations or through the STIB/MIVB app, which also provides real-time updates on schedules and routes. A single ticket is valid for an hour and allows unlimited transfers between metro, tram, and bus services within that time. If you're planning to use public transportation frequently, consider purchasing a day pass or a multi-day pass, which offers unlimited travel and great value for money. Navigating the metro is straightforward, with clear signage and maps available in multiple languages, making it accessible even for first-time visitors.

Taxis and rideshare services are another convenient way to get around Belgium, particularly in cities like Brussels, Antwerp, and Ghent. Taxis are widely available and can be hailed on the street, found at designated taxi stands, or booked through apps like Taxi.eu. Fares are metered, with rates varying depending on the time of day and distance traveled. While taxis are reliable, they can be more expensive than other forms of transportation, so they're best reserved for short trips or late-night journeys when public transport is less frequent. Rideshare services like Uber are also available in major cities, offering a more affordable and flexible alternative to traditional taxis. With Uber, you can book a ride directly through the app, track your driver's location, and pay electronically, making it a hassle-free option. To ensure a smooth experience, always confirm the driver's details and vehicle before getting in, and consider checking fare estimates in advance to avoid surprises.

Public buses are a fantastic way to explore Belgium, especially if you're traveling to smaller towns or rural areas not served by trains or the metro. The bus networks are operated by different companies depending on the region: De Lijn in Flanders, TEC in Wallonia, and STIB/MIVB in Brussels. Buses are frequent, reliable, and well-maintained, making them a practical choice for getting around. Tickets can be purchased at bus stops, on board (though this may cost slightly more), or through the respective apps, which also provide route maps and schedules. In addition to buses, trams are a popular mode of transport in cities like Antwerp and Ghent, offering a scenic and efficient way to travel. While Belgium doesn't have a significant ferry network, walking is an excellent way to explore its compact cities. Many of Belgium's historic centers, such as Bruges and Leuven, are pedestrian-friendly, with cobblestone streets, picturesque squares, and charming canals that are best enjoyed on foot. Walking allows you to soak in the atmosphere, discover hidden gems, and truly connect with the character of each city.

If you're planning to explore Belgium's countryside or visit multiple cities at your own pace, renting a car can be a great option. Major car rental companies like Hertz, Avis, and Europcar have offices in airports and city centers, making it easy to pick up and drop off a vehicle. Rental costs typically range from €40 to €80 per day, depending on the type of car and the rental duration. Driving in Belgium is straightforward, with well-maintained roads and clear signage, but there are a few things to keep in mind. Parking in city centers can be limited and expensive, so it's worth researching parking garages or park-and-ride facilities in advance. Additionally, Belgium has strict traffic laws, including speed limits and regulations for using mobile phones while driving, so be sure to familiarize yourself with the rules before hitting the road. If you're visiting during the winter months, check whether your rental car is equipped with winter tires, as they may be required in certain conditions.

CHAPTER 4
ACCOMMODATION OPTIONS IN BELGIUM

Luxury Accommodations in Bruges, Brussels, Antwerp, and Ghent

Belgium's most iconic cities—Bruges, Brussels, Antwerp, and Ghent—offer a range of luxurious accommodations that combine elegance, comfort, and world-class service. Whether you're looking for a historic hotel steeped in charm, a modern retreat with cutting-edge amenities, or a boutique property with personalized touches, these accommodations promise to make your stay unforgettable. Below are ten exceptional options to consider for your visit.

1. Hotel Dukes' Palace, Bruges

- **Price Range**: Starting at €300 per night.
- **Amenities**: This five-star hotel is housed in a 15th-century ducal residence and features opulent rooms with antique furnishings, marble bathrooms, and modern amenities like free Wi-Fi. Guests can enjoy a tranquil spa with a sauna and steam room, lush gardens, and a gourmet breakfast buffet.

- **Best Area to Stay**: Located in the heart of Bruges, just a short walk from the Markt and the Belfry, this hotel offers unparalleled access to the city's medieval charm.
- **Contact Details**: www.hoteldukespalace.com | +32 50 44 78 88

2. Relais Bourgondisch Cruyce, Bruges

- **Price Range**: Starting at €280 per night.
- **Amenities**: This boutique hotel overlooks the canals and features individually decorated rooms with antique furnishings and luxurious fabrics. Guests can enjoy a

delicious breakfast in the elegant dining room with views of the water.
- **Best Area to Stay**: Nestled along Bruges' picturesque canals, the hotel is centrally located, making it easy to explore the city's enchanting streets and landmarks.
- **Contact Details**: www.relaisbourgondischcruyce.be | +32 50 33 79 26

3. Hotel Amigo, Brussels

- **Price Range**: Starting at €350 per night.
- **Amenities**: This five-star hotel offers stylish rooms with marble bathrooms, plush bedding, and modern amenities. Guests can dine at the Michelin-starred restaurant, relax at the stylish bar, or work out in the fitness center.
- **Best Area to Stay**: Located just steps from the Grand Place, the hotel is ideal for exploring Brussels' top

attractions, including the Manneken Pis and the Royal Palace.
- **Contact Details**: www.roccofortehotels.com | +32 2 547 47 47

4. Steigenberger Wiltcher's, Brussels

- **Price Range**: Starting at €320 per night.
- **Amenities**: This grand hotel features spacious rooms, a fitness center, and fine dining options. Its timeless elegance and impeccable service make it a favorite among luxury travelers.
- **Best Area to Stay**: Situated on the prestigious Avenue Louise, the hotel is perfect for luxury shopping and exploring Brussels' cultural attractions.
- **Contact Details**: www.steigenberger.com | +32 2 542 42 42

5. Hotel Julien, Antwerp

- **Price Range**: Starting at €250 per night.

- **Amenities**: This boutique hotel combines modern design with historic architecture, offering stylish rooms, a rooftop terrace with stunning city views, and a wellness area with a sauna and steam bath.
- **Best Area to Stay**: Located in the city center, near the Cathedral of Our Lady and the vibrant shopping district, the hotel is perfectly positioned for exploring Antwerp.
- **Contact Details**: www.hotel-julien.com | +32 3 229 06 00

6. Hotel FRANQ, Antwerp

- **Price Range**: Starting at €270 per night.
- **Amenities**: Set in a former bank building, this boutique hotel features elegant rooms, a Michelin-starred restaurant, and a cozy bar.
- **Best Area to Stay**: Centrally located, the hotel is close to Antwerp's museums, galleries, and designer boutiques.
- **Contact Details**: www.hotelfranq.com | +32 3 555 31 80

7. Pillows Grand Boutique Hotel Reylof, Ghent

- **Price Range**: Starting at €280 per night.
- **Amenities**: This luxurious retreat is housed in an 18th-century mansion and features elegant rooms, a spa with an indoor pool and sauna, and a fine-dining restaurant.
- **Best Area to Stay**: Located near the historic center, the hotel is an ideal base for exploring Ghent's landmarks, such as Gravensteen Castle and St. Bavo's Cathedral.
- **Contact Details**: www.pillowshotels.com | +32 9 235 40 70

8. 1898 The Post, Ghent

- **Price Range**: Starting at €250 per night.
- **Amenities**: This boutique hotel is located in a historic post office building and features vintage-inspired decor, a cozy cocktail bar, and beautifully designed rooms.
- **Best Area to Stay**: Situated near the Graslei and Korenlei canals, the hotel offers easy access to Ghent's best attractions.
- **Contact Details**: www.1898thepost.com | +32 9 277 16 00

9. The Pand Hotel, Bruges

- **Price Range**: Starting at €240 per night.
- **Amenities**: Housed in an 18th-century carriage house, this boutique hotel features individually decorated rooms, a charming breakfast room, and a library bar.
- **Best Area to Stay**: Located near the canals and the Markt, the hotel is a perfect base for exploring Bruges.
- **Contact Details**: www.pandhotel.com | +32 50 34 06 66

10. Auberge du Pêcheur, Ghent

- **Price Range**: Starting at €220 per night.
- **Amenities**: This elegant hotel is located along the River Lys and features spacious rooms, a gourmet restaurant, and beautiful gardens.

- **Best Area to Stay**: Ideal for those seeking relaxation and natural beauty, while still being close to Ghent's city center.
- **Contact Details**: www.auberge-du-pecheur.be | +32 9 282 31 44

Mid-Range Hotels and Boutique Stays in Bruges, Brussels, Antwerp, and Ghent

Belgium's cities of Bruges, Brussels, Antwerp, and Ghent offer a variety of mid-range hotels and boutique accommodations that combine comfort, charm, and affordability. These options are perfect for travelers who want a memorable stay without splurging on luxury. From cozy boutique hotels in historic buildings to modern properties with thoughtful amenities, these accommodations provide excellent value for money while ensuring a pleasant and convenient experience. Below are ten carefully selected mid-range hotels and boutique stays to consider for your trip.

1. Hotel de Orangerie, Bruges

- **Price Range**: Starting at €180 per night.
- **Amenities**: This charming boutique hotel is set in a 15th-century former convent overlooking the canal. The rooms are elegantly decorated with antique furnishings and modern comforts like free Wi-Fi and flat-screen TVs. Guests can enjoy a delightful breakfast in the dining room or on the terrace by the water.
- **Best Area to Stay**: Located in the heart of Bruges, just steps from the Markt and the Belfry, the hotel offers easy access to the city's main attractions and picturesque streets.
- **Contact Details**: www.hoteldeorangerie.com | +32 50 34 16 49

2. Hotel Jan Brito, Bruges

- **Price Range**: Starting at €150 per night.
- **Amenities**: Housed in a historic building, this boutique hotel features individually styled rooms with period details, a tranquil garden, and a fitness area. A

complimentary breakfast is served daily, and the hotel offers bike rentals for exploring the city.
- **Best Area to Stay**: Situated near the canals and within walking distance of Bruges' historic center, the hotel is perfectly located for sightseeing.
- **Contact Details**: www.janbrito.com | +32 50 33 06 01

3. 9Hotel Sablon, Brussels

- **Price Range**: Starting at €160 per night.
- **Amenities**: This modern boutique hotel offers stylish rooms, a wellness area with a sauna and hot tub, and a cozy lounge for relaxing after a day of exploring. Free Wi-Fi and a daily breakfast buffet are included.
- **Best Area to Stay**: Located in the Sablon district, the hotel is close to art galleries, antique shops, and the Grand Place, making it an excellent base for exploring Brussels.

- **Contact Details**: www.9-hotel-sablon-brussels.be | +32 2 880 07 76

4. Made in Louise, Brussels

- **Price Range**: Starting at €140 per night.
- **Amenities**: This family-run boutique hotel features cozy, individually designed rooms, a charming courtyard, and a billiards room. Guests can enjoy a hearty breakfast and personalized service that makes them feel at home.
- **Best Area to Stay**: Located in a quiet neighborhood near Avenue Louise, the hotel offers a peaceful retreat while still being close to shops, restaurants, and public transportation.
- **Contact Details**: www.madeinlouise.com | +32 2 537 40 33

5. Hotel Rubens-Grote Markt, Antwerp

- **Price Range**: Starting at €170 per night.
- **Amenities**: This boutique hotel offers spacious rooms with modern decor, a complimentary breakfast, and a rooftop terrace with views of the city. Free Wi-Fi and a 24-hour front desk add to the convenience.
- **Best Area to Stay**: Located just steps from the Grote Markt and the Cathedral of Our Lady, the hotel is ideal for exploring Antwerp's historic center.
- **Contact Details**: www.hotelrubensantwerp.com | +32 3 222 48 48

6. Hotel Banks, Antwerp

- **Price Range**: Starting at €130 per night.
- **Amenities**: This trendy boutique hotel features minimalist rooms, a cozy lounge with complimentary drinks and snacks, and a sunny terrace. Breakfast is available, and the hotel offers free Wi-Fi throughout.
- **Best Area to Stay**: Situated in the fashion district, the hotel is close to designer boutiques, art galleries, and the Museum of Contemporary Art.
- **Contact Details**: www.hotelbanks.be | +32 3 304 33 00

7. Hotel Harmony, Ghent

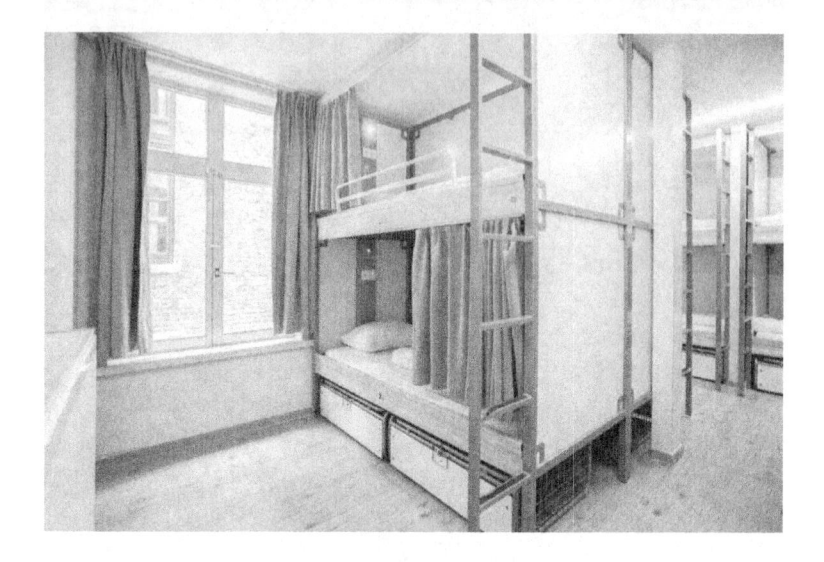

- **Price Range**: Starting at €190 per night.
- **Amenities**: This boutique hotel offers luxurious rooms with canal views, a heated outdoor pool, and a daily breakfast buffet. The hotel also provides free Wi-Fi and a cozy bar for evening drinks.
- **Best Area to Stay**: Located in the historic Patershol district, the hotel is within walking distance of Gravensteen Castle and the Graslei.
- **Contact Details**: www.hotel-harmony.be | +32 9 269 02 02

8. Pillows Boutique Hotel, Ghent

- **Price Range**: Starting at €180 per night.
- **Amenities**: This elegant boutique hotel features stylish rooms, a fine-dining restaurant, and a tranquil garden.

Guests can enjoy personalized service and a relaxing atmosphere.
- **Best Area to Stay**: Situated near the historic center, the hotel is close to St. Bavo's Cathedral and the vibrant Korenmarkt.
- **Contact Details**: www.pillowshotels.com | +32 9 235 40 70

9. Hotel The Peellaert, Bruges

- **Price Range**: Starting at €160 per night.
- **Amenities**: This adults-only hotel offers elegant rooms, a wellness area with a sauna and steam bath, and a complimentary breakfast. The historic building adds to the charm of the stay.
- **Best Area to Stay**: Located in the heart of Bruges, the hotel is just a short walk from the city's main attractions, including the Markt and the canals.
- **Contact Details**: www.thepeellaert.com | +32 50 33 78 89

10. Hotel Carlton, Ghent

- **Price Range**: Starting at €140 per night.
- **Amenities**: This family-run hotel offers spacious rooms, a delicious breakfast, and personalized service. Free Wi-Fi and bike rentals are also available.
- **Best Area to Stay**: Located near the train station, the hotel is convenient for travelers exploring Ghent and other nearby cities.
- **Contact Details**: www.hotelcarlton.be | +32 9 222 88 36

Budget-Friendly Hostels and Guesthouses in Bruges, Brussels, Antwerp, and Ghent

Traveling on a budget doesn't mean you have to sacrifice comfort or convenience. Belgium's cities of Bruges, Brussels, Antwerp, and Ghent offer a variety of affordable hostels and guesthouses that provide clean, comfortable accommodations with plenty of charm. These budget-friendly options are perfect for solo travelers, backpackers, or anyone looking to save money while still enjoying a great stay. Below are ten excellent choices that combine affordability with a welcoming atmosphere and convenient locations.

1. St. Christopher's Inn Hostel, Bruges

- **Price Range**: Starting at €25 per night for a dorm bed, €70 for private rooms.
- **Amenities**: This lively hostel offers free Wi-Fi, a bar with discounted drinks for guests, and a spacious garden for relaxing. Breakfast is available for an additional fee, and the hostel organizes social events to help travelers connect.
- **Best Area to Stay**: Located just a 10-minute walk from the Markt, the hostel is close to Bruges' main attractions, including the Belfry and the canals.
- **Contact Details**: www.st-christophers.co.uk | +32 50 33 80 37

2. Snuffel Hostel, Bruges

- **Price Range**: Starting at €30 per night for a dorm bed, €80 for private rooms.
- **Amenities**: This modern and eco-friendly hostel features free Wi-Fi, a bar, a communal kitchen, and a cozy lounge area. Guests can also rent bikes to explore the city.
- **Best Area to Stay**: Situated in a quiet neighborhood, the hostel is just a short walk from Bruges' historic center, making it a peaceful yet convenient base.
- **Contact Details**: www.snuffel.be | +32 50 33 31 33

3. Sleep Well Youth Hostel, Brussels

- **Price Range**: Starting at €35 per night for a dorm bed, €90 for private rooms.

- **Amenities**: This centrally located hostel offers free Wi-Fi, a complimentary breakfast, and a games room. The modern facilities include a bar and a terrace for socializing.
- **Best Area to Stay**: Located near the city center, the hostel is within walking distance of the Grand Place, shopping streets, and public transportation.
- **Contact Details**: www.sleepwell.be | +32 2 218 50 50

4. Jacques Brel Youth Hostel, Brussels

- **Price Range**: Starting at €30 per night for a dorm bed, €85 for private rooms.
- **Amenities**: This hostel features free Wi-Fi, a bar, a garden terrace, and a complimentary breakfast. It also offers a communal kitchen and regular cultural events.
- **Best Area to Stay**: Situated in the European Quarter, the hostel is close to museums, parks, and public transport links.
- **Contact Details**: www.lesaubergesdejeunesse.be | +32 2 218 01 87

5. Antwerp Central Youth Hostel, Antwerp

- **Price Range**: Starting at €28 per night for a dorm bed, €75 for private rooms.
- **Amenities**: This hostel offers free Wi-Fi, a complimentary breakfast, and a communal lounge. Guests can also enjoy a bar and a terrace.
- **Best Area to Stay**: Located in the heart of Antwerp, the hostel is close to the Cathedral of Our Lady, the Grote Markt, and the city's vibrant nightlife.

- **Contact Details**: www.jeugdherbergen.be | +32 3 234 03 14

6. Boomerang Hostel, Antwerp

- **Price Range**: Starting at €20 per night for a dorm bed, €60 for private rooms.
- **Amenities**: This budget-friendly hostel features free Wi-Fi, a communal kitchen, and a cozy lounge with a fireplace. The relaxed atmosphere makes it a great place to meet other travelers.
- **Best Area to Stay**: Situated near Antwerp's city center, the hostel is within walking distance of museums, shops, and public transport.

- **Contact Details**: www.boomeranghostel.com | +32 3 281 56 00

7. Hostel Uppelink, Ghent

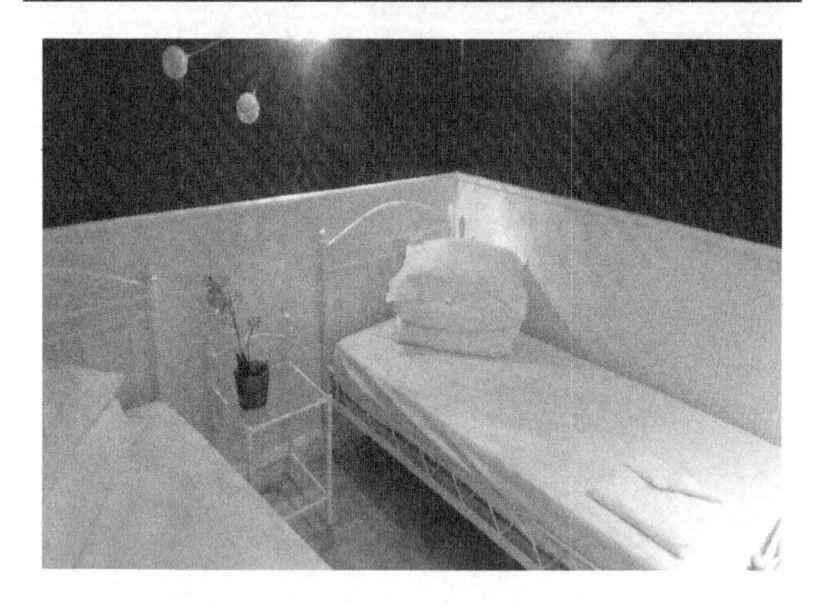

- **Price Range**: Starting at €25 per night for a dorm bed, €70 for private rooms.
- **Amenities**: This riverside hostel offers free Wi-Fi, a bar, and a communal kitchen. Guests can also rent kayaks to explore the canals.
- **Best Area to Stay**: Located in the historic center, the hostel is close to Gravensteen Castle, the Graslei, and St. Bavo's Cathedral.
- **Contact Details**: www.hosteluppelink.com | +32 9 279 44 77

8. Treck Hostel, Ghent

- **Price Range**: Starting at €30 per night for a dorm bed, €80 for private rooms.
- **Amenities**: This unique hostel features themed caravans as sleeping quarters, along with free Wi-Fi, a bar, and a communal kitchen. Guests can also enjoy a garden and a games room.
- **Best Area to Stay**: Situated just outside the city center, the hostel offers a quirky and fun experience while still being close to Ghent's main attractions.
- **Contact Details**: www.treckhostel.be | +32 9 395 52 39

9. Hostel Lybeer, Bruges

- **Price Range**: Starting at €25 per night for a dorm bed, €70 for private rooms.
- **Amenities**: This cozy hostel offers free Wi-Fi, a bar, and a communal kitchen. The friendly staff organizes social events, making it easy to meet fellow travelers.
- **Best Area to Stay**: Located in the city center, the hostel is within walking distance of Bruges' top attractions, including the Markt and the canals.
- **Contact Details**: www.hostellybeer.com | +32 50 34 10 93

10. Hostel 47, Ghent

- **Price Range**: Starting at €22 per night for a dorm bed, €65 for private rooms.
- **Amenities**: This budget-friendly hostel features free Wi-Fi, a communal kitchen, and a garden terrace. The

relaxed atmosphere is perfect for budget-conscious travelers.
- **Best Area to Stay**: Located near the city center, the hostel is close to public transport and Ghent's historic landmarks.
- **Contact Details**: www.hostel47.com | +32 9 233 46 47

CHAPTER 5
DINING IN BELGIUM

Belgium is a country that takes its food seriously, offering a culinary experience that is as rich and diverse as its history. From iconic dishes like waffles and fries to world-class restaurants and vibrant food markets, Belgium's dining scene caters to every taste and budget. Whether you're indulging in a luxurious meal, enjoying a hearty plate of traditional fare, or sampling local beers at a historic brewery, Belgium's culinary offerings promise to leave you with unforgettable memories.

Famous Belgian Foods: Waffles, Chocolate, Fries, and More

Belgium is home to some of the world's most iconic foods, and no visit is complete without sampling these culinary treasures.

1. Belgian Waffles

Belgium is famous for its waffles, which come in two main varieties: the light and crispy Brussels waffle and the dense, caramelized Liège waffle. Brussels waffles are typically served with powdered sugar, whipped cream, or fresh fruit, while Liège waffles are sweet on their own, thanks to chunks of pearl sugar that caramelize during cooking. For the best waffles, visit **Maison Dandoy** in Brussels (www.maisondandoy.com) or **Chez Albert** in Bruges.

2. Belgian Chocolate

Belgium is world-renowned for its chocolate, and pralines—delicate, filled chocolates—are a national specialty. Visit iconic chocolatiers like **Neuhaus**, **Pierre Marcolini**, and **Leonidas** to sample some of the finest Belgian chocolate. Many shops also offer tours and workshops, giving you a behind-the-scenes look at the chocolate-making process.

3. Belgian Fries (Frites)

Belgian fries are a national obsession, known for their crispy exterior and fluffy interior. They're traditionally served in a paper cone with a variety of sauces, including the classic mayonnaise. For some of the best fries, head to **Maison Antoine** in Brussels or **Frituur No. 1** in Antwerp.

4. Carbonnade Flamande

This hearty Flemish beef stew is slow-cooked in Belgian beer, giving it a rich, slightly sweet flavor. It's often served with fries or crusty bread. Try it at **De Vlaamsche Pot** in Bruges or **Le Marmiton** in Brussels.

5. Moules-Frites (Mussels and Fries)

A quintessential Belgian dish, moules-frites features fresh mussels steamed in a flavorful broth of white wine, garlic, and herbs, paired with golden fries. Enjoy this classic at **Chez Léon** in Brussels or **Den Dyver** in Bruges.

Restaurants by Price Range

Belgium's dining scene offers something for everyone, from high-end gourmet experiences to cozy mid-range bistros and budget-friendly eateries.

Luxury Dining

- **Hof van Cleve (Kruisem)**: A three-Michelin-star restaurant offering innovative Belgian cuisine. Prices start at €250 per person. Reservations are essential (www.hofvancleve.com).
- **Comme Chez Soi (Brussels)**: A two-Michelin-star restaurant known for its elegant French-Belgian cuisine. Prices start at €150 per person (www.commechezsoi.be).

Mid-Range Restaurants

- **De Vlaamsche Pot (Bruges)**: A cozy restaurant serving traditional Flemish dishes like carbonnade flamande and waterzooi. Prices range from €25 to €40 per person (www.devlaamschepot.be).
- **Balls & Glory (Ghent)**: A modern eatery specializing in stuffed meatballs and hearty sides. Prices range from €15 to €25 per person (www.ballsnglory.be).

Budget-Friendly Eateries

- **Fritland (Brussels)**: A popular spot for Belgian fries, located near the Grand Place. A generous portion of fries with sauce costs around €5 (www.fritland.be).
- **Waffle Factory (Multiple Locations)**: Perfect for a quick and affordable waffle fix, with prices starting at €4 (www.wafflefactory.com).

Street Food Recommendations and Food Markets

Belgium's street food scene is vibrant and diverse, offering everything from crispy fries to sweet waffles and savory snacks. Food markets are also a great way to sample local flavors and experience the country's culinary culture.

Street Food Highlights

- **Belgian Fries**: Known locally as "frites," these twice-fried potatoes are a national obsession. Look

for friteries (fry stands) like **Maison Antoine** in Brussels or **Frituur No. 1** in Antwerp for some of the best fries in the country. Prices range from €3 to €6.
- **Liège Waffles**: These dense, caramelized waffles are a must-try. Vendors like **Chez Albert** in Bruges or **Vitalgaufre** in Brussels serve some of the best.

Food Markets

- **Brussels' Sunday Market at Gare du Midi**: One of the largest markets in Belgium, offering everything from fresh produce to international street food. It's a lively spot to grab a quick bite or shop for local ingredients.
- **Vrijdagmarkt (Ghent)**: Held every Friday, this market features local produce, cheeses, and baked goods, as well as food stalls serving traditional Belgian snacks.
- **Antwerp Exotic Market**: Located at Theaterplein, this market is a melting pot of flavors, with vendors offering everything from Moroccan pastries to Belgian specialties.

Best Breweries and Trappist Beers

Belgium is a beer lover's paradise, home to some of the world's finest breweries and Trappist beers. These beers are brewed by monks in monasteries, following centuries-old traditions.

1. Westvleteren Brewery (Sint-Sixtus Abbey)

Known for producing some of the world's best beer, Westvleteren is a must-visit for beer enthusiasts. The brewery's Westvleteren 12 is legendary for its rich, complex flavor. Reservations are required to purchase beer (www.sintsixtus.be).

2. Cantillon Brewery (Brussels)

This family-run brewery specializes in lambic beers, known for their sour and fruity flavors. Visitors can tour the brewery and sample their unique creations (www.cantillon.be).

3. Chimay Brewery (Scourmont Abbey)

Chimay is one of Belgium's most famous Trappist breweries, offering a range of beers that pair perfectly with their artisanal cheeses. The abbey also has a visitor center and tasting room (www.chimay.com).

4. De Halve Maan Brewery (Bruges)

Located in the heart of Bruges, this historic brewery offers guided tours and tastings of their popular Brugse Zot and Straffe Hendrik beers (www.halvemaan.be).

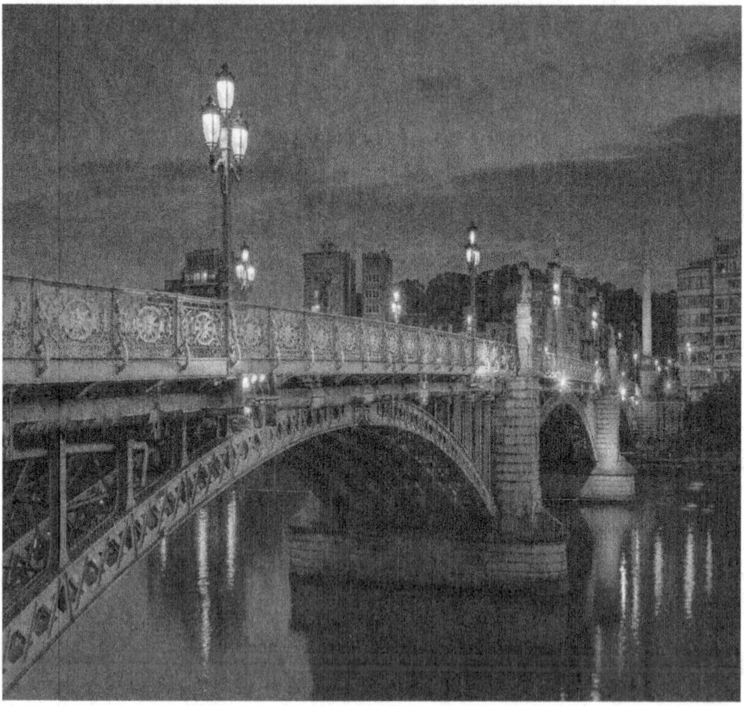

CHAPTER 6
TOP TOURIST ATTRACTIONS IN BELGIUM

Bruges: Canals, Belfry, and the Markt

Bruges, often called the "Venice of the North," is one of Belgium's most enchanting cities, and its historic center feels like stepping into a fairytale. With its picturesque canals, medieval architecture, and cobblestone streets, Bruges offers a wealth of attractions that captivate visitors from around the world. Among its many highlights, the canals, the Belfry, and the Markt stand out as must-visit destinations. Here's everything you need to know to plan your visit to these iconic attractions.

The Canals of Bruges

The canals of Bruges are the lifeblood of the city, winding through its historic center and offering stunning views of medieval buildings reflected in the water. Originally built for trade and transportation, the canals are now one of Bruges' most iconic features, earning the city its nickname. Exploring the canals is a magical experience that allows you to see Bruges from a unique perspective.

- **Why Visit**: A boat tour along the canals is one of the best ways to take in the beauty of Bruges. You'll glide past historic landmarks, charming bridges, and hidden gardens, all while learning about the city's history from a knowledgeable guide.
- **Activities**: Take a 30-minute guided boat tour, available from several departure points around the city, including near the Rozenhoedkaai, one of Bruges' most photographed spots.
- **Entry Prices**: Boat tours cost approximately €12 per person, with discounts for children. Tickets can be purchased on-site or in advance through local tour operators.
- **Best Visiting Times**: Early morning or late afternoon tours are ideal for avoiding crowds and enjoying the canals in a quieter, more serene atmosphere.

- **Contact Information**: For more details, visit www.visitbruges.be.

The Belfry of Bruges (Belfort)

Standing tall in the heart of Bruges, the Belfry is one of the city's most recognizable landmarks. This medieval bell tower, dating back to the 13th century, offers breathtaking views of the city and a glimpse into Bruges' rich history.

- **Why Visit**: Climbing the Belfry's 366 steps is a rewarding experience, as it leads to a panoramic view of Bruges and its surrounding countryside. Along the way, you'll pass the carillon, a set of 47 bells that still chime today, and learn about the tower's role in the city's history.
- **Activities**: Visitors can explore the tower's interior, including the treasury room, which once housed important city documents. The highlight, of course, is reaching the top for the stunning views.
- **Entry Prices**: Tickets cost €14 for adults, €12 for seniors, and €8 for children aged 6-25. Children under 6 enter for free. Tickets can be purchased on-site or online in advance to skip the line.
- **Best Visiting Times**: Visit early in the morning or late in the afternoon to avoid long queues, especially during peak tourist seasons.
- **Contact Information**: For tickets and more information, visit www.museabrugge.be.

The Markt

The Markt, or Market Square, is the vibrant heart of Bruges, surrounded by colorful gabled buildings, cafes, and historic landmarks. This bustling square has been the center of city life for centuries and remains a lively gathering place for locals and visitors alike.

- **Why Visit**: The Markt is the perfect spot to soak in the atmosphere of Bruges. Whether you're admiring the architecture, enjoying a meal at one of the many outdoor cafes, or simply people-watching, the square offers a quintessential Bruges experience.
- **Activities**: Explore the square's highlights, including the Provincial Court and the Historium, an

interactive museum that brings Bruges' medieval history to life. On Wednesdays, the square hosts a traditional market where you can shop for local produce, flowers, and crafts.
- **Entry Prices**: Access to the Markt is free, but entry to the Historium costs €15 for adults, €13 for seniors, and €10 for children aged 3-12. Combination tickets with a virtual reality experience are also available.
- **Best Visiting Times**: Visit in the morning to enjoy the square before it gets too crowded, or come in the evening to see it beautifully lit up.
- **Contact Information**: For more information about the Historium, visit www.historium.be.

Brussels: Grand Place, Atomium, and European Parliament

Brussels, the vibrant capital of Belgium, is a city that seamlessly blends history, culture, and modernity. From its breathtaking medieval square to futuristic architecture and the heart of European politics, Brussels offers a variety of attractions that cater to every type of traveler. Among its many highlights, the **Grand Place**, **Atomium**, and **European Parliament** stand out as must-visit destinations. Here's everything you need to know to plan your visit to these iconic attractions.

Grand Place

The Grand Place, or Grote Markt, is the crown jewel of Brussels and one of the most beautiful squares in the world. Surrounded by ornate guildhalls, the Town Hall, and the King's House (Maison du Roi), this UNESCO World Heritage Site is a masterpiece of Gothic and Baroque architecture.

- **Why Visit**: The Grand Place is a feast for the eyes, with its intricate facades and golden details. It's the perfect spot to soak in the history and grandeur of

Brussels. The square is also the site of major events, such as the biennial Flower Carpet, where the square is covered in a stunning floral display.

- **Activities**: Stroll through the square to admire the architecture, visit the Town Hall for a guided tour, or explore the Museum of the City of Brussels in the King's House to learn about the city's history. Don't forget to grab a coffee or Belgian beer at one of the nearby cafes while enjoying the lively atmosphere.
- **Entry Prices**: Access to the square is free. Guided tours of the Town Hall cost €10 for adults and €8 for students and seniors. Entry to the Museum of the City of Brussels costs €8 for adults, €6 for seniors, and €4 for students.
- **Best Visiting Times**: Visit early in the morning or in the evening to avoid crowds and enjoy the square's magical ambiance when it's illuminated at night.
- **Contact Information**: For more details, visit www.brussels.be.

Atomium

The Atomium is one of Brussels' most iconic landmarks, a futuristic structure built for the 1958 World Expo. Shaped like an iron crystal magnified 165 billion times, the Atomium is both a museum and an architectural marvel.

- **Why Visit**: The Atomium offers a unique combination of art, science, and breathtaking views. Its nine interconnected spheres house exhibitions, and the top sphere features a panoramic observation deck with stunning views of Brussels and beyond.

- **Activities**: Explore the permanent and temporary exhibitions inside the spheres, which focus on science, design, and the history of the Atomium. Take the elevator to the top sphere for panoramic views, and enjoy a meal or drink at the restaurant located there.
- **Entry Prices**: Tickets cost €16 for adults, €14 for seniors, and €8.50 for children aged 6-17. Children under 6 enter for free. Combination tickets with Mini-Europe, a nearby attraction, are also available. Tickets can be purchased online in advance to skip the line.

- **Best Visiting Times**: Visit early in the morning or late in the afternoon to avoid peak crowds. Weekdays are generally quieter than weekends.
- **Contact Information**: For tickets and more information, visit www.atomium.be.

European Parliament

As the political heart of the European Union, the European Parliament is a fascinating place to learn about the workings of the EU and its impact on Europe and the world. Located in the European Quarter, this modern complex is both an architectural and cultural highlight of Brussels.

- **Why Visit**: The European Parliament offers a unique opportunity to delve into European politics and history. The Parlamentarium, the Parliament's visitor center, features interactive exhibits that make learning about the EU engaging and accessible.
- **Activities**: Take a self-guided tour of the Parlamentarium, where you can explore exhibits on the history of the EU, its member states, and how decisions are made. You can also visit the Hemicycle, the Parliament's debating chamber, to see where key decisions are made. Guided tours are available in multiple languages.
- **Entry Prices**: Admission to the European Parliament and the Parlamentarium is free. Guided tours of the Hemicycle are also free but require advance booking.
- **Best Visiting Times**: Visit during weekdays when the Parliament is in session for a chance to see the Hemicycle in action. Mornings are generally quieter than afternoons.
- **Contact Information**: For more details and to book tours, visit www.europarl.europa.eu.

Antwerp: Cathedral of Our Lady, Rubens House, and Diamond District

Antwerp, Belgium's second-largest city, is a vibrant destination known for its rich history, artistic heritage, and status as the diamond capital of the world. Whether you're admiring the grandeur of its Gothic cathedral, stepping into the world of a Baroque master, or exploring the glittering Diamond District, Antwerp offers a wealth of attractions that will leave you inspired. Here's everything you need to know about visiting the **Cathedral of Our Lady**, **Rubens House**, and **Diamond District**.

Cathedral of Our Lady (Onze-Lieve-Vrouwekathedraal)

The Cathedral of Our Lady is a masterpiece of Gothic architecture and one of Antwerp's most iconic landmarks. Towering over the city at 123 meters, it is the tallest church in Belgium and a UNESCO World Heritage Site. Inside, the cathedral houses an impressive collection of art, including several works by the renowned Baroque painter Peter Paul Rubens.

- **Why Visit**: The cathedral is a stunning example of Gothic architecture, with intricate details, soaring arches, and beautiful stained-glass windows. Its art collection, including Rubens' masterpieces such as *The Descent from the Cross* and *The Assumption of the Virgin Mary*, makes it a must-visit for art and history enthusiasts.
- **Activities**: Explore the cathedral's interior, admire its art collection, and learn about its history through informative displays. Guided tours are available for those who want a deeper understanding of the cathedral's significance.
- **Entry Prices**: Tickets cost €12 for adults, €10 for seniors, and €6 for students. Children under 12 enter for free. Tickets can be purchased on-site or online in advance.
- **Best Visiting Times**: Visit early in the morning or late in the afternoon to avoid crowds, especially during weekends and holidays.
- **Contact Information**: For more details and tickets, visit www.dekathedraal.be.

Rubens House (Rubenshuis)

The Rubens House is the former home and studio of Peter Paul Rubens, one of the most celebrated Baroque painters in history. This beautifully restored 17th-century mansion offers a glimpse into the life and work of the artist, showcasing his masterpieces and personal collection.

- **Why Visit**: The Rubens House is both a museum and a historic site, where you can walk in the footsteps of the artist and see where he created some of his most famous works. The house is filled with original paintings, sculptures, and period furnishings, offering a fascinating insight into Rubens' world.
- **Activities**: Tour the house and studio, admire Rubens' artwork and personal collection, and explore the lush garden, which has been restored to its original design. Audio guides and guided tours are available to enhance your visit.
- **Entry Prices**: Tickets cost €12 for adults, €8 for seniors and students, and €1 for children aged 12-25. Children under 12 enter for free. Tickets can be purchased online to secure your spot.
- **Best Visiting Times**: Weekday mornings are the best time to visit for a quieter experience. The museum can get busy on weekends and during peak tourist seasons.
- **Contact Information**: For tickets and more information, visit www.rubenshuis.be.

Diamond District

Antwerp's Diamond District is the epicenter of the global diamond trade, with over 80% of the world's rough diamonds passing through this area. Located near the Central

Station, the district is a fascinating place to learn about the history and craftsmanship of diamonds.

- **Why Visit**: The Diamond District offers a unique opportunity to explore Antwerp's glittering heritage. You can visit diamond shops, learn about the diamond trade, and even see master craftsmen at work. The district is also home to the **DIVA**

Museum, which showcases the history of diamonds, jewelry, and luxury goods.
- **Activities**: Stroll through the district to browse diamond shops and admire the dazzling displays. Visit the DIVA Museum to learn about the history of diamonds and see exquisite jewelry collections. The museum also offers interactive exhibits and workshops.
- **Entry Prices**: Entry to the DIVA Museum costs €12 for adults, €10 for seniors, and €8 for students. Children under 12 enter for free. Tickets can be purchased online or at the museum.
- **Best Visiting Times**: Visit during weekdays to see the district at its busiest, as this is when the diamond trade is in full swing. The DIVA Museum is less crowded in the late afternoon.
- **Contact Information**: For more information about the DIVA Museum, visit www.divaantwerp.be.

Ghent: Gravensteen Castle, St. Bavo's Cathedral, and the Graslei

Ghent is a city that effortlessly combines medieval charm with a vibrant, modern atmosphere. Known for its stunning architecture, rich history, and lively canals, Ghent is a must-visit destination in Belgium. Among its many attractions, **Gravensteen Castle**, **St. Bavo's Cathedral**, and the **Graslei** stand out as highlights that showcase the city's unique character. Here's everything you need to know to plan your visit to these iconic landmarks.

Gravensteen Castle (Castle of the Counts)

Gravensteen Castle, or the Castle of the Counts, is a striking medieval fortress that dominates the heart of Ghent. Built in the 12th century, this imposing structure served as the residence of the Counts of Flanders and later as a courthouse, prison, and even a factory. Today, it's one of the best-preserved castles in Belgium and a fascinating window into the city's past.

- **Why Visit**: Gravensteen Castle is a must-see for history enthusiasts and anyone who loves exploring medieval architecture. Its thick stone walls, towers, and battlements transport you back in time, offering a glimpse into the lives of the Flemish nobility.

- **Activities**: Explore the castle's interior, including the Great Hall, dungeons, and armory, which houses a collection of medieval weapons and armor. Climb to the top of the castle for panoramic views of Ghent's historic center. The castle also features an engaging audio guide narrated with humor and storytelling, making the experience both educational and entertaining.

- **Entry Prices**: Tickets cost €12 for adults, €7 for students and seniors, and €2 for children aged 6-12. Children under 6 enter for free. Tickets can be purchased online in advance to skip the line.
- **Best Visiting Times**: Visit early in the morning or late in the afternoon to avoid crowds, especially during weekends and holidays.
- **Contact Information**: For tickets and more information, visit www.gravensteen.stad.gent.

St. Bavo's Cathedral (Sint-Baafskathedraal)

St. Bavo's Cathedral is a masterpiece of Gothic architecture and one of Ghent's most important religious landmarks. It is best known as the home of the **Ghent Altarpiece**, also called *The Adoration of the Mystic Lamb*, a world-famous painting by the Van Eyck brothers.

- **Why Visit**: The cathedral is a stunning example of Gothic design, with soaring arches, intricate stained-glass windows, and a rich history that dates back to the 10th century. The Ghent Altarpiece, considered one of the most influential works of art in Western history, is a must-see for art lovers.

- **Activities**: Admire the cathedral's stunning interior, including its ornate chapels and crypt. Visit the dedicated viewing area for the Ghent Altarpiece, where you can marvel at its intricate details and learn about its fascinating history through an audio guide. Guided tours of the cathedral are also available.
- **Entry Prices**: Entry to the cathedral is free, but tickets to view the Ghent Altarpiece cost €12 for adults, €10 for seniors, and €2 for children aged 6-12. Children under 6 enter for free. Tickets can be purchased online or at the cathedral.
- **Best Visiting Times**: Mornings are the best time to visit for a quieter experience, especially if you want to spend time admiring the Ghent Altarpiece without crowds.
- **Contact Information**: For more details and tickets, visit www.sintbaafskathedraal.be.

The Graslei

The Graslei is one of the most picturesque spots in Ghent, a historic quay lined with beautifully preserved medieval buildings that reflect in the waters of the Leie River. This area was once the center of Ghent's medieval trade and remains a lively hub for locals and visitors alike.

- **Why Visit**: The Graslei is the perfect place to soak in the charm of Ghent. Its stunning architecture, vibrant atmosphere, and scenic views make it a favorite spot for photography, relaxing, and people-watching.

- **Activities**: Take a leisurely stroll along the quay to admire the historic buildings, many of which date back to the 12th century. Enjoy a meal or drink at one of the many cafes and restaurants with outdoor seating, offering views of the river. For a unique perspective, hop on a boat tour that departs from the Graslei and explore Ghent's canals.
- **Entry Prices**: Access to the Graslei is free. Boat tours cost approximately €10-€12 per person, with

discounts for children. Tickets can be purchased on-site or through local tour operators.

- **Best Visiting Times**: Visit in the late afternoon or early evening to enjoy the golden hour, when the light creates a magical ambiance. The Graslei is also particularly beautiful at night when the buildings are illuminated.
- **Contact Information**: For more information about boat tours and activities, visit www.visitgent.be.

Hidden Gems and Lesser-Known Attractions in Belgium

While Belgium is famous for its iconic landmarks like the Grand Place, Atomium, and Bruges' canals, the country is also home to a wealth of hidden gems and lesser-known attractions that offer unique and unforgettable experiences. These off-the-beaten-path destinations provide a deeper look into Belgium's history, culture, and natural beauty, making them perfect for curious travelers seeking something different. Here are some of Belgium's best-kept secrets to add to your itinerary.

Hallerbos (The Blue Forest)

Located just outside Brussels, Hallerbos is a magical forest that comes alive every spring when a carpet of bluebells blooms, creating a breathtaking sea of purple and blue. This natural wonder is a must-visit for nature lovers and photographers.

- **Why Visit**: Hallerbos is one of the most enchanting forests in Europe, especially during the bluebell season in April and May. The vibrant colors and serene atmosphere make it a perfect escape from the city.
- **Activities**: Take a leisurely walk along the well-marked trails, enjoy a picnic in the forest, or capture stunning photos of the bluebells. Guided tours are available during the blooming season to learn more about the forest's ecology.
- **Entry Prices**: Entry to the forest is free. Guided tours may have a small fee, depending on the provider.
- **Best Visiting Times**: Visit early in the morning on weekdays during the bluebell season to avoid crowds and enjoy the forest at its most peaceful.
- **Contact Information**: For more details, visit www.hallerbos.be.

Dinant and the Collegiate Church of Notre Dame

Nestled along the Meuse River, the charming town of Dinant is a hidden gem known for its dramatic cliffs, picturesque views, and the stunning Collegiate Church of Notre Dame.

It's also the birthplace of Adolphe Sax, the inventor of the saxophone.

- **Why Visit**: Dinant's unique setting, with its colorful buildings and towering cliffs, is unlike anywhere else in Belgium. The Collegiate Church of Notre Dame, with its striking Gothic architecture and onion-shaped bell tower, is a highlight of the town.
- **Activities**: Explore the church's beautiful interior, take a cable car ride to the Citadel of Dinant for panoramic views, and visit the Adolphe Sax Museum to learn about the history of the saxophone. You can also enjoy a boat ride along the Meuse River.
- **Entry Prices**: Entry to the church is free. Tickets for the Citadel and cable car cost €11 for adults, €9 for students and seniors, and €7 for children.

- Combination tickets for the Citadel and boat rides are also available.
- **Best Visiting Times**: Visit in the late afternoon to enjoy the golden light on the cliffs and river. Weekdays are quieter than weekends.
- **Contact Information**: For more information, visit www.dinant.be.

The Abbey of Villers-la-Ville

The Abbey of Villers-la-Ville is a stunning ruin of a Cistercian abbey that dates back to the 12th century. Surrounded by lush greenery, the abbey is a peaceful and atmospheric site that offers a glimpse into Belgium's monastic history.

- **Why Visit**: The abbey's dramatic ruins, with their soaring arches and crumbling walls, are a photographer's dream. The site is steeped in history and offers a tranquil setting for exploration.
- **Activities**: Wander through the ruins, visit the herb garden, and learn about the abbey's history through interactive exhibits. The abbey also hosts cultural events, such as concerts and light shows, throughout the year.
- **Entry Prices**: Tickets cost €9 for adults, €7 for seniors and students, and €4 for children aged 6-12. Children under 6 enter for free. Tickets can be purchased online or at the entrance.
- **Best Visiting Times**: Visit in the morning or late afternoon to enjoy the site in a quieter, more serene atmosphere.
- **Contact Information**: For tickets and more details, visit www.villers.be.

The Underground Caves of Han (Grottes de Han)

Located in the Ardennes region, the Caves of Han are one of Europe's most impressive underground cave systems. These natural wonders are part of a UNESCO Global Geopark and offer a fascinating journey into the depths of the earth.

- **Why Visit**: The caves are a geological marvel, with stunning stalactites, stalagmites, and underground rivers. The guided tours are both educational and awe-inspiring, making them a great experience for all ages.

- **Activities**: Take a guided tour of the caves, visit the wildlife park that's part of the same complex, and explore the museum dedicated to the region's natural history.
- **Entry Prices**: Combination tickets for the caves and wildlife park cost €29 for adults, €22 for children aged 4-11, and are free for children under 4. Tickets can be purchased online in advance.
- **Best Visiting Times**: Visit early in the day to join the first tours and avoid peak crowds, especially during weekends and school holidays.

- **Contact Information**: For tickets and more information, visit www.grotte-de-han.be.

The Beguinages of Belgium

The beguinages are serene, enclosed communities that were once home to religious women known as Beguines. These UNESCO World Heritage Sites are scattered across Belgium, with some of the most beautiful examples in Bruges, Leuven, and Mechelen.

- **Why Visit**: The beguinages are peaceful oases in the heart of bustling cities, offering a glimpse into a unique way of life. Their whitewashed houses, cobblestone streets, and tranquil gardens make them perfect for a quiet stroll.
- **Activities**: Walk through the beguinages to admire their architecture and learn about their history. Some sites, like the Beguinage in Bruges, also have small museums.
- **Entry Prices**: Entry is free for most beguinages, though some museums may charge a small fee (around €5).
- **Best Visiting Times**: Visit in the morning or early evening for a peaceful experience, as these sites are often less crowded than other attractions.
- **Contact Information**: For more information, visit www.visitflanders.com.

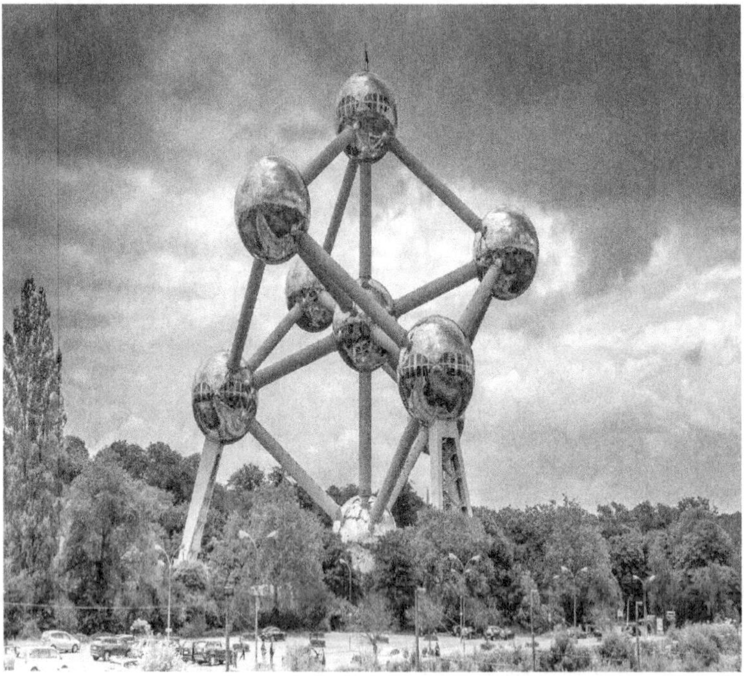

CHAPTER 7
CULTURAL EXPERIENCES IN BELGIUM

Art and Architecture: Flemish Masters and Art Nouveau

Belgium is a treasure trove of artistic and architectural wonders, offering a journey through centuries of creativity and innovation. From the timeless works of the Flemish Masters to the elegant curves of Art Nouveau, the country's art and architecture reflect its rich cultural heritage and enduring influence on the world.

Flemish Masters: A Legacy of Genius

The Flemish Masters—artists like Jan van Eyck, Pieter Bruegel the Elder, and Peter Paul Rubens—are among the most celebrated painters in European history. Their works, created during the 15th to 17th centuries, are renowned for their technical mastery, attention to detail, and ability to capture the human experience with unparalleled depth and emotion.

3. Jan van Eyck

Jan van Eyck, often considered the father of oil painting, revolutionized art with his use of light, texture, and realism. His most famous work, *The Adoration of the Mystic Lamb* (commonly known as the Ghent Altarpiece), is a masterpiece of religious art and a must-see for any visitor to Belgium.

- **Where to See It**: The Ghent Altarpiece is housed in **St. Bavo's Cathedral** in Ghent. Tickets to view the altarpiece cost €12 for adults, €10 for seniors, and €2 for children aged 6-12. Visit www.sintbaafskathedraal.be for more information.
- **Best Visiting Times**: Mornings are ideal for a quieter experience, especially during weekdays.

2. Pieter Bruegel the Elder

Known for his vivid depictions of peasant life and landscapes, Pieter Bruegel the Elder's works are both visually stunning and rich in social commentary. His paintings, such as *The Harvesters* and *The Peasant Wedding*, offer a glimpse into 16th-century life.

- **Where to See It**: The **Royal Museums of Fine Arts of Belgium** in Brussels houses several of Bruegel's masterpieces. Tickets cost €15 for adults, €10 for seniors, and €5 for students. Visit www.fine-arts-museum.be for details.

- **Best Visiting Times**: Late afternoons are quieter, and the museum is less crowded during weekdays.

3. Peter Paul Rubens

Rubens, a master of the Baroque style, is celebrated for his dramatic compositions, vibrant colors, and dynamic figures. His works often depict mythological and religious themes, showcasing his extraordinary talent and imagination.

- **Where to See It**: Visit the **Rubens House** in Antwerp, the artist's former home and studio, to see his works and learn about his life. Tickets cost €12 for adults, €8 for seniors and students, and €1 for children aged 12-25. Visit www.rubenshuis.be for more information.
- **Best Visiting Times**: Weekday mornings are the best time to visit for a quieter experience.

Art Nouveau: Elegance in Design

At the turn of the 20th century, Belgium became a hub for the Art Nouveau movement, a style characterized by flowing lines, organic forms, and intricate details. Architects like Victor Horta and Paul Hankar transformed the urban landscape with their innovative designs, creating buildings that are as functional as they are beautiful.

4. Victor Horta's Masterpieces

Victor Horta is considered one of the pioneers of Art Nouveau architecture. His buildings are known for their harmonious integration of structure and decoration, with features like curved ironwork, stained glass, and intricate mosaics.

- **Where to See It**: The **Horta Museum** in Brussels, located in Horta's former home and studio, is a stunning example of his work. Tickets cost €12 for

adults, €6 for students, and €4 for children aged 6-12. Visit www.hortamuseum.be for details.
- **Best Visiting Times**: Visit early in the morning or late in the afternoon to avoid crowds.

2. Maison Autrique

Designed by Victor Horta, Maison Autrique is one of the earliest examples of Art Nouveau architecture. This beautifully restored house offers a glimpse into the origins of the movement.

- **Where to See It**: Maison Autrique is located in Brussels. Tickets cost €10 for adults and €6 for students and seniors. Visit www.autrique.be for more information.

- **Best Visiting Times**: Weekdays are generally quieter than weekends.

3. Stoclet Palace

The Stoclet Palace, a UNESCO World Heritage Site, is a masterpiece of Art Nouveau and early modernist design. Designed by Austrian architect Josef Hoffmann, the palace is a private residence and not open to the public, but its exterior is worth admiring.

- **Where to See It**: The palace is located in the Woluwe-Saint-Pierre district of Brussels. While you can't enter, you can view the exterior from the street.
- **Best Visiting Times**: Visit during daylight hours to fully appreciate the intricate details of the I.

Combining Art and Architecture

Belgium's art and architecture are deeply intertwined, with many museums and galleries housed in historic buildings that are works of art in themselves. For example, the **Royal Greenhouses of Laeken** in Brussels combine Art Nouveau design with lush botanical displays, while the **Museum aan de Stroom (MAS)** in Antwerp offers stunning views of the city alongside its diverse exhibits.

Festivals and Events: Carnival, Ommegang, and More

Belgium is a country that knows how to celebrate, with a calendar full of vibrant festivals and events that showcase its rich traditions, history, and culture. From centuries-old parades to lively carnivals, these celebrations offer a unique way to experience the heart and soul of Belgium. Whether you're drawn to colorful costumes, historical reenactments, or lively music and dance, Belgium's festivals promise unforgettable memories. Here's a closer look at some of the country's most iconic events, including **Carnival**, **Ommegang**, and more.

Carnival in Binche

The Carnival of Binche is one of Belgium's most famous and unique festivals, recognized by UNESCO as a Masterpiece of the Oral and Intangible Heritage of Humanity. This centuries-old celebration takes place in the small town of Binche and is known for its elaborate costumes, lively parades, and traditional rituals.

- **Why Visit**: The highlight of the carnival is the appearance of the **Gilles**, men dressed in elaborate costumes with feathered hats and wax masks. They parade through the streets, throwing oranges to the crowd as a symbol of good luck. The atmosphere is electric, with music, dancing, and fireworks adding to the festivities.

- **When It Happens**: The Carnival of Binche takes place during the three days leading up to Ash Wednesday, with the main events occurring on Shrove Tuesday.
- **Entry Prices**: The event is free to attend, but it's recommended to arrive early to secure a good spot for the parades.
- **Best Visiting Times**: Shrove Tuesday is the best day to experience the carnival in full swing, but the festivities on the preceding days are also worth attending.
- **Contact Information**: For more details, visit www.carnavaldebinche.be.

Ommegang in Brussels

The Ommegang is a spectacular historical pageant that takes place in the heart of Brussels, recreating the grand procession held in 1549 to honor Emperor Charles V. This event is a celebration of Brussels' rich history and heritage, featuring hundreds of participants in period costumes.

- **Why Visit**: The Ommegang is a feast for the senses, with knights, musicians, dancers, and horses parading through the streets of Brussels. The

highlight is the reenactment in the **Grand Place**, where the square is transformed into a medieval spectacle with music, lights, and performances.
- **When It Happens**: The Ommegang is held annually in early July, over two evenings.
- **Entry Prices**: Tickets for the Grand Place seating range from €40 to €80, depending on the location. Standing areas around the city are free to access. Tickets can be purchased online in advance.
- **Best Visiting Times**: Arrive early to secure a good viewing spot, especially if you're attending the free-standing areas. The evening performances in the Grand Place are the highlight of the event.
- **Contact Information**: For tickets and more information, visit www.ommegang.be.

Gentse Feesten (Ghent Festival)

The Gentse Feesten is one of Europe's largest cultural festivals, transforming the city of Ghent into a lively hub of music, theater, and street performances. This 10-day event attracts millions of visitors and offers something for everyone.

- **Why Visit**: The festival features a diverse lineup of events, including concerts, comedy shows, art exhibitions, and children's activities. The streets come alive with food stalls, pop-up bars, and street performers, creating a festive atmosphere.

- **When It Happens**: The Gentse Feesten takes place every July, starting on the Friday before the third Sunday of the month.
- **Entry Prices**: Most events and performances are free, though some concerts and shows may require tickets.
- **Best Visiting Times**: Visit during the evenings to experience the festival at its liveliest, with music and performances continuing late into the night.
- **Contact Information**: For schedules and more details, visit www.gentsefeesten.be.

Zinneke Parade in Brussels

The Zinneke Parade is a biennial event that celebrates Brussels' diversity and creativity. This colorful parade features community groups from across the city, showcasing their talents through imaginative costumes, music, and performances.

- **Why Visit**: The Zinneke Parade is a unique, non-commercial event that highlights the multicultural spirit of Brussels. Each edition has a different theme, inspiring participants to create innovative and thought-provoking displays.
- **When It Happens**: The parade takes place every two years in May.
- **Entry Prices**: The event is free to attend.
- **Best Visiting Times**: Arrive early to secure a good viewing spot along the parade route.

- **Contact Information**: For more details, visit www.zinneke.org.

Rock Werchter

Rock Werchter is one of Europe's most renowned music festivals, attracting top international artists and thousands of music fans to the small village of Werchter. This four-day festival offers an unforgettable experience for music lovers.

- **Why Visit**: The festival features a stellar lineup of rock, pop, and indie artists, along with a vibrant festival atmosphere. With multiple stages, food trucks, and camping options, it's a must-visit for music enthusiasts.
- **When It Happens**: Rock Werchter takes place annually in late June or early July.
- **Entry Prices**: Tickets start at €127 for a single day and €292 for a four-day pass. Camping passes are available for an additional fee. Tickets sell out quickly, so it's best to book early.
- **Best Visiting Times**: Arrive early each day to explore the festival grounds and secure a good spot for your favorite performances.
- **Contact Information**: For tickets and more information, visit www.rockwerchter.be.

Flower Carpet in Brussels

Every two years, the Grand Place in Brussels is transformed into a stunning floral display during the Flower Carpet event. This l creation features over 500,000 begonias arranged in intricate patterns, celebrating Belgium's horticultural heritage.

- **Why Visit**: The Flower Carpet is a visual masterpiece, offering a rare opportunity to see the Grand Place in a completely new light. The event also includes concerts and light shows, adding to the magical atmosphere.
- **When It Happens**: The Flower Carpet is held every two years in mid-August.
- **Entry Prices**: Viewing the carpet from the square is free. Tickets to access the Town Hall balcony for a panoramic view cost €5.
- **Best Visiting Times**: Visit in the early morning or late evening to avoid crowds and enjoy the best lighting for photos.
- **Contact Information**: For more details, visit www.flowercarpet.be.

Belgian Etiquette and Customs

When visiting Belgium, understanding the local etiquette and customs can help you navigate the country with ease and show respect for its culture. Belgians value politeness, discretion, and respect for others, and following these norms will ensure a positive experience during your trip.

Tipping Norms

Tipping in Belgium is generally more relaxed compared to some other countries, as service charges are often included in the price of goods and services. However, there are still situations where tipping is appreciated or customary.

5. Dining at Restaurants

- **Standard Practice**: In most restaurants, a service charge is already included in the bill, so tipping is not mandatory. However, it's common to round up the bill or leave a small tip as a gesture of appreciation for good service.
- **Percentage Guidelines**: If you wish to tip, rounding up to the nearest €5 or €10 is sufficient for casual dining. For fine dining or exceptional service, leaving 5-10% of the bill is appreciated but not expected.
- **How to Tip**: You can leave the tip in cash on the table or hand it directly to the server. If paying by card, check if there's an option to add a tip.

2. Taxi Rides

- **Standard Practice**: Tipping taxi drivers is not obligatory, but rounding up the fare to the nearest euro or adding €1-€2 is a common courtesy, especially for longer rides or if the driver assists with luggage.
- **How to Tip**: Simply hand the driver the rounded-up amount in cash or let them keep the change.

3. Hotel Staff

- **Standard Practice**: Tipping hotel staff is appreciated but not expected. For example, you might tip €1-€2 per bag for porters or leave €1-€2 per night for housekeeping staff.
- **How to Tip**: Leave cash in an envelope or on the bedside table for housekeeping, and hand tips directly to porters or other staff.

4. Tour Guides

- **Standard Practice**: Tipping tour guides is customary, especially for private or small-group tours. A tip of €5-€10 per person for a half-day tour or €10-€20 for a full-day tour is appropriate.
- **How to Tip**: Hand the tip directly to the guide at the end of the tour, preferably in cash.

5. Discretionary Tipping

- In Belgium, tipping is generally seen as a discretionary act of gratitude rather than an obligation. If you're unsure whether to tip, rounding up the bill or leaving a small amount is always a safe and appreciated gesture.

Expected Behavior in Public Spaces

Belgians are known for their politeness and respect for others, and these values are reflected in their expectations for behavior in public. Here are some key cultural norms to keep in mind:

6. Respectful Conduct

- **Noise Levels**: Belgians value quiet and peaceful environments, especially in public spaces like trains, buses, and restaurants. Keep your voice at a moderate level and avoid loud or disruptive behavior.
- **Queuing**: Belgians are orderly when it comes to queuing. Always wait your turn in line, whether at a shop, ticket counter, or public transport stop. Cutting in line is considered rude.
- **Interactions with Locals**: Politeness is highly valued. Always greet people with a friendly "Bonjour" (French-speaking areas) or "Goedendag"

(Dutch-speaking areas) before starting a conversation. Saying "please" (*s'il vous plaît* or *alstublieft*) and "thank you" (*merci* or *dank u wel*) is essential.

2. Dress Codes

- **General Attire**: Belgians tend to dress smartly and appreciate neat, well-put-together outfits. Casual clothing is acceptable for sightseeing, but avoid overly revealing or sloppy attire.
- **Religious and Cultural Sites**: When visiting churches, cathedrals, or other religious sites, dress modestly. Avoid wearing shorts, tank tops, or hats inside these spaces. A scarf or shawl can be useful for covering shoulders if needed.

3. Photography Etiquette

- **Public Areas**: Taking photos in public spaces is generally acceptable, but always be mindful of others. Avoid photographing people without their permission, especially in close-up shots.
- **Private Areas**: In museums, galleries, or religious sites, check for signage indicating whether photography is allowed. Flash photography is often prohibited to protect artworks.
- **How to Seek Permission**: If you want to photograph someone or a private property, politely ask for

permission first. A simple "May I take a photo?" (*Puis-je prendre une photo?* Or *Mag ik een foto maken?*) is appreciated.

4. Customs and Traditions

- **Greetings**: A handshake is the standard greeting in Belgium, especially in formal or professional settings. Among friends or close acquaintances, three kisses on the cheek (alternating sides) is common, though this varies by region.
- **Gestures to Avoid**: Avoid pointing at people, as it can be considered impolite. Additionally, refrain from making jokes about Belgium's linguistic or cultural differences, as these can be sensitive topics.
- **Dining Etiquette**: When dining with locals, wait for the host to start eating or toasting before you begin. It's also polite to keep your hands visible on the table (but not your elbows).

Language Tips: Dutch, French, and English

Belgium is a multilingual country with three official languages: Dutch, French, and German. The majority of Belgians speak either Dutch or French, depending on the region, while German is spoken by a smaller community in the east. English is widely understood, especially in cities and tourist areas, but learning a few key phrases in Dutch and French can go a long way in making your trip more enjoyable and showing respect for the local culture. Here's a guide to navigating Belgium's linguistic landscape.

Understanding Belgium's Language Regions

Belgium is divided into three main language regions:

- **Flanders (Dutch-speaking)**: In the northern part of Belgium, Dutch (often referred to as Flemish) is the primary language. Cities like Antwerp, Ghent, and Bruges are in this region.
- **Wallonia (French-speaking)**: In the southern part of Belgium, French is the dominant language. Cities like Namur, Liège, and Mons are located here.
- **Brussels (Bilingual)**: The capital city, Brussels, is officially bilingual, with both Dutch and French widely spoken. However, French is more commonly used in daily life.
- **German-speaking Community**: A small region in eastern Belgium near the German border speaks German as its primary language.

Key Phrases in Dutch and French

Learning a few basic phrases in Dutch and French can help you navigate Belgium more easily and make a positive impression on locals. Here are some essential phrases to get you started:

Greetings and Politeness

- **Hello**:
    - Dutch: *Hallo* or *Goedendag*
    - French: *Bonjour*
- **Goodbye**:
    - Dutch: *Tot ziens*
    - French: *Au revoir*
- **Please**:
    - Dutch: *Alstublieft*
    - French: *S'il vous plaît*
- **Thank you**:
    - Dutch: *Dank u wel*
    - French: *Merci*
- **You're welcome**:
    - Dutch: *Graag gedaan*
    - French: *De rien*
- **Excuse me / Sorry**:
    - Dutch: *Excuseer* or *Sorry*
    - French: *Excusez-moi* or *Pardon*

Asking for Help

- **Do you speak English?**
  - Dutch: *Spreekt u Engels?*
  - French: *Parlez-vous anglais?*
- **I don't understand**:
  - Dutch: *Ik begrijp het niet*
  - French: *Je ne comprends pas*
- **Where is…?**
  - Dutch: *Waar is…?*
  - French: *Où est…?*
- **How much does it cost?**
  - Dutch: *Hoeveel kost het?*
  - French: *Combien ça coûte?*

Numbers (1-10)

- **Dutch**: Eén, Twee, Drie, Vier, Vijf, Zes, Zeven, Acht, Negen, Tien
- **French**: Un, Deux, Trois, Quatre, Cinq, Six, Sept, Huit, Neuf, Dix

Using English in Belgium

English is widely spoken in Belgium, especially in major cities like Brussels, Antwerp, and Bruges, as well as in tourist areas. Many Belgians, particularly younger generations, are fluent in English and happy to communicate with you. However, it's always polite to start a conversation with a greeting in Dutch or French before switching to English. For example:

- In Flanders: *"Goedendag! Spreekt u Engels?"*
- In Wallonia: *"Bonjour! Parlez-vous anglais?"*

Tips for Navigating Belgium's Multilingualism

1. **Know the Region**: Be aware of the language spoken in the region you're visiting. In Flanders, use Dutch greetings, while in Wallonia, use French. In Brussels, either language is acceptable, though French is more commonly used.
2. **Be Polite**: Belgians appreciate politeness and effort. Even if your pronunciation isn't perfect, locals will appreciate your attempt to speak their language.
3. **Carry a Phrasebook or App**: Having a phrasebook or a translation app like Google Translate can be helpful for quick translations or when you're in less touristy areas.
4. **Look for Multilingual Signs**: In tourist areas, signs and menus are often available in Dutch, French, and English, making it easier to navigate.
5. **Ask for Help**: If you're unsure which language to use, start with English or politely ask which language the person prefers.

Cultural Notes on Language

- **Switching Languages**: Belgians are used to switching between languages, but it's important to respect their linguistic preferences. Avoid assuming that everyone speaks French in Flanders or Dutch in Wallonia.
- **Pronunciation**: Belgian Dutch (Flemish) has a softer accent compared to Dutch spoken in the Netherlands, and Belgian French has its own regional nuances. Don't worry too much about perfect pronunciation—locals will appreciate your effort regardless.
- **Language Sensitivity**: Language can be a sensitive topic in Belgium due to historical and cultural differences between the regions. Avoid making jokes or comments about the language divide.

CHAPTER 8

ADVENTURE AND OUTDOOR ACTIVITIES

Belgium may be known for its charming cities and rich history, but it also offers a wealth of outdoor activities that allow you to connect with nature, enjoy thrilling adventures, or simply relax in beautiful surroundings. Whether you're hiking through lush forests, kayaking along scenic rivers, or exploring botanical gardens, Belgium's outdoor experiences cater to every type of traveler. Here's a guide to the best outdoor activities in Belgium, divided into categories to help you plan your adventure.

Hiking and Nature Walks

Belgium's diverse landscapes make it a fantastic destination for hiking and nature walks. From dense forests to rolling hills and dramatic cliffs, there's a trail for every level of adventurer.

1. High Fens (Hautes Fagnes)

- **Why Visit**: The High Fens, located in the Ardennes region, is Belgium's largest nature reserve and a paradise for hikers. Its unique moorland landscape,

wooden boardwalks, and serene atmosphere make it a must-visit.
- **Trail Highlights**: Popular trails include the **Poleur Walk** (easy, 5 km) and the **Signal de Botrange Trail** (moderate, 10 km), which takes you to Belgium's highest point.
- **Amenities**: Parking, restrooms, and picnic areas are available at the main entrances.
- **Entry Fees**: Free to enter, but guided tours may have a small fee.
- **Contact Information**: Visit www.hautesfagnes.be for maps and guided tour bookings.

2. Sonian Forest (Forêt de Soignes)

- **Why Visit**: Just outside Brussels, this UNESCO-listed beech forest offers peaceful trails perfect for a nature escape.
- **Trail Highlights**: The **Red Trail** (easy, 5 km) is ideal for families, while the **Blue Trail** (moderate, 10 km) offers more challenging terrain.
- **Amenities**: Restrooms, parking, and picnic spots are available.
- **Entry Fees**: Free.
- **Contact Information**: Visit www.sonianforest.be for trail maps and visitor information.

3. Ninglinspo Trail

- **Why Visit**: This picturesque trail follows the Ninglinspo River, with waterfalls, wooden bridges, and natural pools along the way.
- **Trail Highlights**: The loop trail is 6 km and moderately challenging, with plenty of scenic spots for photos.
- **Amenities**: Parking is available at the trailhead, but there are no restrooms, so plan accordingly.
- **Entry Fees**: Free.
- **Contact Information**: Visit www.ardenne.org for more details.

Water-Based Activities

Belgium's rivers, canals, and coastline offer plenty of opportunities for water-based adventures, from kayaking to relaxing boat tours.

1. Kayaking on the Lesse River

- **Why Visit**: The Lesse River in the Ardennes is perfect for a scenic kayaking trip, with gentle rapids, limestone cliffs, and castles along the way.
- **Details**: Kayak trips range from 12 km (2-3 hours) to 21 km (4-5 hours).

- **Costs**: Rentals start at €20 per person, including equipment.
- **Safety Tips**: Life jackets are provided, and children must be accompanied by an adult.
- **Contact Information**: Book with **Dinant Evasion** at www.dinant-evasion.be.

2. Boat Tours in Bruges

- **Why Visit**: Explore Bruges' picturesque canals on a guided boat tour, offering a unique perspective of the city's medieval architecture.
- **Details**: Tours last about 30 minutes and operate from March to November.
- **Costs**: Tickets cost €12 for adults and €6 for children.
- **Contact Information**: Tickets can be purchased at the docks or online at www.visitbruges.be.

3. Belgian Coast Beaches

- **Why Visit**: Belgium's coastline offers sandy beaches and charming seaside towns like Knokke-Heist and De Haan, perfect for a relaxing day by the sea.
- **Activities**: Sunbathing, swimming, and beachside dining. Some beaches also offer paddleboard and windsurfing rentals.

- **Costs**: Free access to beaches; equipment rentals start at €15 per hour.
- **Contact Information**: Visit www.belgiancoast.co.uk for more details.

Adventure Sports

For thrill-seekers, Belgium offers a range of adventure sports, from zip-lining to mountain biking.

7. Rock Climbing in Freyr

- **Why Visit**: Freyr, near Dinant, is Belgium's premier rock-climbing destination, with limestone cliffs overlooking the Meuse River.
- **Details**: Routes range from beginner to advanced, with heights up to 120 meters.
- **Costs**: Guided climbing sessions start at €50 per person, including equipment.
- **Safety Tips**: Always climb with proper gear and a certified guide if you're a beginner.
- **Contact Information**: Book with **Climbing Adventure** at www.climbingadventure.be.

2. Zip-Lining and Rope Courses at Adventure Valley Durbuy

- **Why Visit**: This adventure park in Durbuy offers zip-lining, rope courses, and other adrenaline-pumping activities.

- **Costs**: Day passes start at €35 for adults and €25 for children.
- **Safety Tips**: All activities include safety briefings and equipment.
- **Contact Information**: Visit www.adventure-valley.be for tickets and reservations.

3. Cycling in Limburg

- **Why Visit**: Limburg is known as Belgium's cycling paradise, with scenic routes like the **Cycling Through Water** trail, where you ride through a pond at eye level with the water.
- **Costs**: Bike rentals start at €15 per day.
- **Contact Information**: Visit www.visitlimburg.be for maps and rental options.

Relaxed Outdoor Experiences

If you prefer a slower pace, Belgium offers plenty of opportunities to unwind and enjoy its natural beauty.

1. Meise Botanic Garden

- **Why Visit**: One of the largest botanical gardens in the world, Meise Botanic Garden features over 18,000 plant species and a stunning greenhouse complex.
- **Costs**: Tickets cost €9 for adults and €2 for children.

- **Best Times to Visit**: Spring and summer are ideal for blooming flowers.
- **Contact Information**: Visit www.plantentuinmeise.be.

2. Scenic Drives in the Ardennes

- **Why Visit**: The Ardennes region offers picturesque drives through rolling hills, dense forests, and charming villages.
- **Highlights**: Stop at viewpoints, castles, and local markets along the way.
- **Costs**: Free, though parking fees may apply at some stops.

3. Outdoor Markets

- **Why Visit**: Belgium's outdoor markets, like the **Sunday Market at Gare du Midi** in Brussels, are perfect for browsing fresh produce, flowers, and local crafts.
- **Costs**: Free to enter; prices vary by vendor.
- **Best Times to Visit**: Mornings are the best time to explore markets before they get crowded.

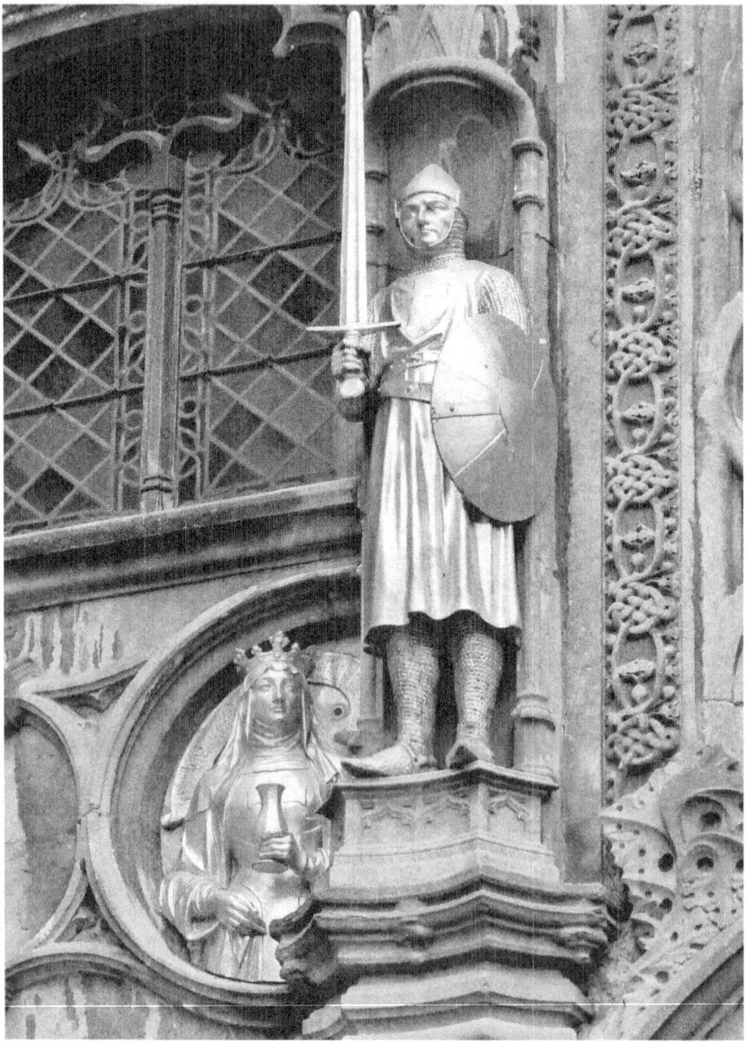

CHAPTER 9
NIGHTLIFE IN BELGIUM

When the sun sets, Belgium comes alive with a vibrant and diverse nightlife scene that caters to every taste. Whether you're in the mood for a laid-back evening at a cozy pub, dancing the night away at a buzzing club, or enjoying live music in an intimate venue, Belgium's nightlife has something for everyone. From trendy neighborhoods to iconic venues, here's your guide to experiencing the best of Belgium after dark.

Popular Venues

Belgium is home to a variety of nightlife hotspots, each offering a unique experience. Here are some of the most notable venues to check out:

1. Delirium Café (Brussels)

- **Type of Entertainment**: Famous for its extensive beer menu, Delirium Café offers over 2,000 types of beer, including rare Belgian brews. The lively atmosphere and rustic décor make it a must-visit for beer enthusiasts.
- **Entry Fees**: Free entry; beer prices range from €4 to €10 depending on the brew.

- **Additional Features**: Regular beer tastings and themed nights.
- **Contact Information**: www.deliriumcafe.be | +32 2 514 44 34

2. Fuse (Brussels)

- **Type of Entertainment**: One of Belgium's most iconic nightclubs, Fuse is a haven for electronic music lovers, hosting world-class DJs and unforgettable techno nights.
- **Entry Fees**: Cover charges range from €10 to €25, depending on the event.
- **Additional Features**: Multiple dance floors, VIP areas, and a cutting-edge sound system.
- **Contact Information**: www.fuse.be | +32 2 511 97 89

3. Café d'Anvers (Antwerp)

- **Type of Entertainment**: Located in a former church, this legendary nightclub is known for its house and techno music, attracting top DJs from around the world.
- **Entry Fees**: Tickets range from €10 to €20.
- **Additional Features**: Unique architecture, a spacious dance floor, and a vibrant crowd.
- **Contact Information**: www.cafedanvers.com

4. Hot Club de Gand (Ghent)

- **Type of Entertainment**: A cozy jazz bar tucked away in a hidden courtyard, Hot Club de Gand offers live jazz performances in an intimate setting.
- **Entry Fees**: Free entry; drinks start at €5.
- **Additional Features**: Outdoor seating in the courtyard and a relaxed, bohemian vibe.
- **Contact Information**: www.hotclubdegand.be

5. Spirito (Brussels)

- **Type of Entertainment**: An upscale nightclub housed in a converted church, Spirito is known for its luxurious décor, high-energy parties, and exclusive atmosphere.
- **Entry Fees**: Cover charges start at €20; VIP packages are available.
- **Additional Features**: Bottle service, themed nights, and a dress code (smart casual).
- **Contact Information**: www.spirito-brussels.com

6. Bonnefooi (Brussels)

- **Type of Entertainment**: A lively bar and music venue offering eclectic live performances, from funk and soul to indie and electronic.
- **Entry Fees**: Free entry; drinks start at €4.

- **Additional Features**: Late-night hours and a laid-back, artsy vibe.
- **Contact Information**: www.bonnefooi.be

Best Neighborhoods for Nightlife Activities

Belgium's cities are home to vibrant neighborhoods that come alive after dark, each offering a unique atmosphere and variety of venues. Here are some of the best areas to explore:

1. Brussels: Saint-Géry and Ixelles

- **Atmosphere**: Saint-Géry is trendy and buzzing, with a mix of bars, clubs, and cafes housed in historic buildings. Ixelles offers a more eclectic vibe, with a mix of upscale lounges and bohemian hangouts.
- **Types of Venues**: Saint-Géry is perfect for bar-hopping, while Ixelles is known for its cocktail bars and live music venues.
- **Convenience**: Both neighborhoods are easily accessible by public transport, and taxis are readily available late at night.
- **Safety Tips**: Stick to well-lit areas and travel in groups if possible.

2. Antwerp: Het Zuid and the Old Town

- **Atmosphere**: Het Zuid is Antwerp's artsy district, known for its stylish bars and cultural venues. The Old Town offers a mix of historic charm and lively nightlife, with plenty of pubs and clubs.
- **Types of Venues**: Het Zuid is ideal for a sophisticated evening, while the Old Town is great for a more casual night out.
- **Convenience**: Both areas are walkable, and public transport runs late into the night.
- **Safety Tips**: Keep an eye on your belongings, especially in crowded areas.

3. Ghent: Patershol and Overpoortstraat

- **Atmosphere**: Patershol is a charming, historic neighborhood with cozy bars and intimate music venues. Overpoortstraat, on the other hand, is a lively student area with affordable pubs and clubs.
- **Types of Venues**: Patershol is perfect for a relaxed evening, while Overpoortstraat is ideal for a high-energy night out.
- **Convenience**: Both areas are easily accessible by tram or on foot.
- **Safety Tips**: Overpoortstraat can get rowdy on weekends, so stay aware of your surroundings.

4. Leuven: Oude Markt

- **Atmosphere**: Known as the "longest bar in the world," Oude Markt is a lively square lined with bars and cafes, making it a hotspot for nightlife.
- **Types of Venues**: From traditional Belgian pubs to modern cocktail bars, there's something for everyone.
- **Convenience**: The square is centrally located and easy to reach by train or bus.
- **Safety Tips**: The area is generally safe, but it's best to avoid walking alone late at night.

5. Bruges: The Historic Center

- **Atmosphere**: While Bruges is quieter than other cities, its historic center offers a selection of charming pubs and bars with a relaxed vibe.
- **Types of Venues**: Enjoy a Belgian beer at a traditional pub or sip cocktails at a stylish lounge.
- **Convenience**: The city center is compact and walkable, making it easy to explore on foot.
- **Safety Tips**: Bruges is very safe, but be mindful of your belongings in busy areas.

CHAPTER 10
SHOPPING IN BELGIUM

Belgium is a shopper's paradise, offering everything from high-end boutiques and designer stores to charming markets and unique local products. Whether you're looking for luxury fashion, artisanal goods, or delicious Belgian treats, the country's shopping scene has something for everyone.

What to Buy in Belgium

Belgium is known for its high-quality products and unique souvenirs. Here are some must-buy items to take home:

1. Belgian Chocolate

- Belgium is world-famous for its chocolate, and no trip is complete without sampling or buying some. Look for pralines (filled chocolates) from iconic chocolatiers like **Neuhaus**, **Pierre Marcolini**, **Leonidas**, and **Godiva**.
- **Where to Buy**: Visit flagship stores in Brussels, Bruges, or Antwerp, or explore smaller artisanal chocolatiers for unique flavors.

2. Belgian Beer

- With over 1,500 varieties of beer, Belgium is a haven for beer lovers. Trappist beers, lambics, and gueuzes are particularly popular.
- **Where to Buy**: Specialty beer shops like **Beer Planet** in Brussels or **De Bier Tempel** in Bruges offer a wide selection.

3. Lace and Tapestry

- Belgian lace is renowned for its intricate craftsmanship, while tapestries are a nod to the country's medieval heritage.
- **Where to Buy**: Bruges is the best place for authentic lace, with shops like **Kantcentrum** offering handmade pieces. For tapestries, visit **Maison de la Tapisserie** in Brussels.

4. Diamonds

- Antwerp is the diamond capital of the world, making it the perfect place to shop for high-quality diamonds and jewelry.
- **Where to Buy**: The **Antwerp Diamond District** is home to hundreds of diamond dealers and jewelers.

5. Fashion and Design

- Belgium is known for its avant-garde fashion designers, such as Dries Van Noten and Ann Demeulemeester. You'll also find unique home décor and design items.

- **Where to Buy**: Antwerp's **ModeNatie** district is a hub for fashion, while Brussels' **Sablon** area offers chic boutiques.

6. Speculoos and Waffles

- Speculoos (spiced cookies) and Belgian waffles make for delicious souvenirs.
- **Where to Buy**: Supermarkets like **Delhaize** or specialty shops like **Maison Dandoy** in Brussels.

Where to Shop in Belgium

Belgium offers a variety of shopping experiences, from bustling markets to luxury shopping streets. Here are some of the best places to shop:

1. Avenue Louise (Brussels)

- **What to Expect**: This upscale shopping street is lined with luxury boutiques, designer stores, and high-end brands like Louis Vuitton, Chanel, and Hermès.
- **Highlights**: Perfect for luxury shopping and window shopping.
- **Tips**: Visit during sales periods (January and July) for discounts on designer items.

2. Meir (Antwerp)

- **What to Expect**: Antwerp's main shopping street, Meir, is a mix of international brands, department stores, and local shops.
- **Highlights**: Don't miss the **Stadsfeestzaal**, a stunning shopping center housed in a historic building.
- **Tips**: Arrive early to avoid crowds, especially on weekends.

3. Rue Neuve (Brussels)

- **What to Expect**: A bustling pedestrian street with popular high-street brands like Zara, H&M, and Primark.
- **Highlights**: Affordable shopping in the heart of Brussels.
- **Tips**: Combine your visit with a stop at the nearby **City2 Shopping Mall**.

4. Bruges Markets

- **What to Expect**: Bruges is known for its charming markets, where you can shop for lace, chocolates, and other local products.
- **Highlights**: The **Wednesday Market** at the Markt Square is a great spot for fresh produce and souvenirs.
- **Tips**: Bring cash, as some vendors may not accept cards.

5. Maasmechelen Village

- **What to Expect**: A luxury outlet shopping village offering discounts on designer brands like Prada, Gucci, and Burberry.
- **Highlights**: Great for bargain hunters looking for high-end fashion.
- **Tips**: Visit during weekdays for a quieter shopping experience.

6. Sablon (Brussels)

- **What to Expect**: This chic neighborhood is known for its antique shops, art galleries, and artisanal chocolate stores.
- **Highlights**: Perfect for unique finds and luxury gifts.
- **Tips**: Explore the area on weekends to enjoy the **Sablon Antiques Market**.

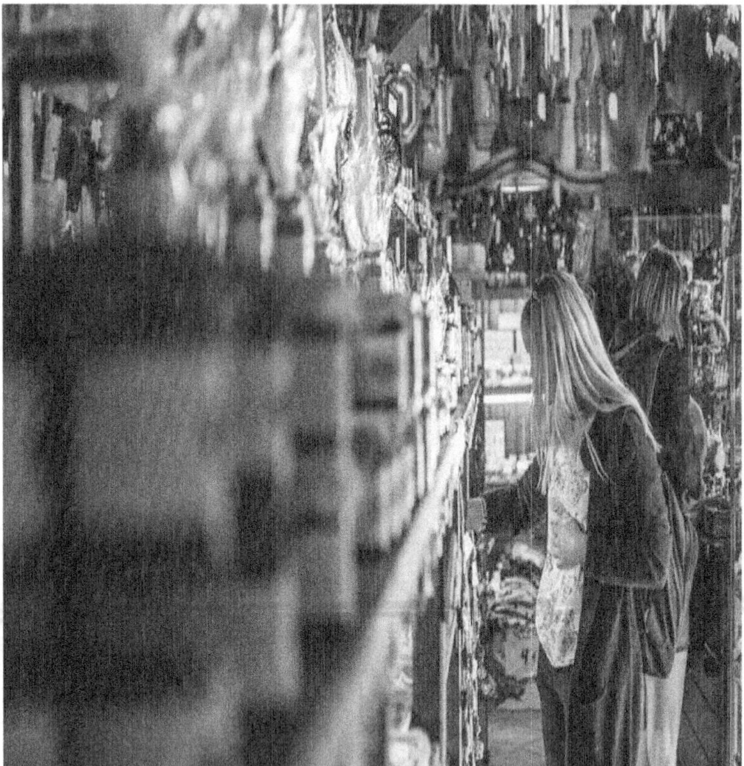

CHAPTER 11
SAFETY AND EMERGENCY INFORMATION

Belgium is a safe and welcoming country for travelers, but like any destination, it's important to stay aware of your surroundings and be prepared for unexpected situations. Whether you're exploring bustling markets, navigating public transportation, or visiting popular tourist attractions, a little preparation can go a long way in ensuring a safe and enjoyable trip. Here's a comprehensive guide to staying safe and knowing what to do in case of an emergency while in Belgium.

Safety Tips for Crowded Areas

Belgium's cities and tourist hotspots, such as Brussels, Bruges, and Antwerp, can get quite busy, especially during peak travel seasons. Here are some practical tips to help you stay safe in crowded areas:

1. Protecting Personal Belongings

- **Guard Against Pickpockets**: Pickpocketing can occur in crowded places like markets, train stations, and tourist attractions. Keep your valuables secure by

using a money belt or an anti-theft bag with zippers. Avoid keeping wallets or phones in back pockets.
- **Be Mindful of Bags**: Always keep your bag in front of you, especially in crowded areas or on public transportation. If you're sitting at a café or restaurant, loop your bag strap around your chair or keep it on your lap.
- **Avoid Flashing Valuables**: Refrain from displaying expensive jewelry, cameras, or large amounts of cash, as this can attract unwanted attention.

2. Navigating Crowds

- **Avoid Rush Hours**: Public transportation in cities like Brussels and Antwerp can get very crowded during rush hours (7:30–9:30 AM and 4:30–6:30 PM). Plan your travel outside these times if possible.
- **Stay Aware of Your Surroundings**: Be mindful of your surroundings and avoid distractions like using your phone while walking in busy areas. This will help you stay alert to potential risks.
- **Have a Meeting Point**: If you're traveling with others, agree on a meeting point in case you get separated in a crowd.

3. Staying Connected

- **Share Your Itinerary**: Let someone you trust know your travel plans, including where you're staying and your daily itinerary.
- **Keep Your Phone Charged**: Always carry a fully charged phone and, if possible, a portable charger. Save important numbers, such as your hotel and emergency contacts, in your phone.
- **Use Local Apps**: Download apps like **Google Maps** for navigation and **112 BE** (Belgium's official emergency app) for real-time safety updates and emergency assistance.

Emergency Contact Information

In case of an emergency, it's important to know who to contact and where to go for help. Here's a list of essential emergency contact numbers and resources in Belgium:

1. Police and Medical Services

- **Emergency Number (Police, Fire, Ambulance)**: Dial **112** for immediate assistance in any emergency. This number is free and works across the European Union.
- **Non-Emergency Police Assistance**: Dial **101** for non-urgent police matters.

2. Embassies and Consulates

If you lose your passport, need legal assistance, or require help from your home country, contact your embassy or consulate. Here are some major embassies in Belgium:

- **United States Embassy (Brussels)**:
    - Phone: +32 2 811 4000
    - Website: be.usembassy.gov
- **United Kingdom Embassy (Brussels)**:
    - Phone: +32 2 287 62 11
    - Website: www.gov.uk/world/belgium
- **Canadian Embassy (Brussels)**:
    - Phone: +32 2 741 06 11
    - Website: www.canadainternational.gc.ca
- **Australian Embassy (Brussels)**:
    - Phone: +32 2 286 05 00

- Website: www.belgium.embassy.gov.au

3. Helplines for Tourists

- **Tourist Assistance Hotline**: Dial **+32 2 513 77 44** for general tourist information and assistance.
- **Anti-Poison Center**: Dial **070 245 245** for help in case of poisoning or chemical exposure.

4. Hospitals and Medical Facilities

Belgium has excellent healthcare facilities, and many doctors and staff speak English. Here are some reputable hospitals:

- **UZ Brussel (Brussels)**:
    - Phone: +32 2 477 41 11
    - Website: www.uzbrussel.be
- **CHU Brugmann (Brussels)**:
    - Phone: +32 2 477 21 11
    - Website: www.chu-brugmann.be
- **AZ Sint-Jan (Bruges)**:
    - Phone: +32 50 45 21 11
    - Website: www.azsintjan.be

5. Local Apps and Services

- **112 BE App**: Belgium's official emergency app allows you to call emergency services and share your

location with responders. It's free to download and highly recommended for travelers.
- **SafeAround**: This app provides safety ratings and tips for neighborhoods in Belgium and other countries.

CHAPTER 12
DAY TRIP RECOMMENDATIONS

Belgium's compact size and excellent transportation network make it an ideal base for exploring nearby destinations. Whether you're staying in Bruges, Brussels, Antwerp, or Ghent, you'll find a variety of charming towns, historic landmarks, and scenic landscapes just a short journey away. From picturesque villages to cultural treasures, these day trips offer a perfect escape from the city while immersing you in Belgium's rich heritage and natural beauty.

Nearby Destinations

From Bruges, a visit to **Damme** and the **Belgian Coast** is a delightful way to spend the day. Damme, a quaint medieval village just 7 kilometers from Bruges, is known for its charming canals, historic buildings, and literary heritage. You can stroll along the cobblestone streets, visit the Church of Our Lady, or enjoy a leisurely bike ride along the canal that connects Damme to Bruges. The Belgian Coast, with its sandy beaches and seaside towns like Knokke-Heist, offers a relaxing retreat. You can sunbathe, explore the dunes, or indulge in fresh seafood at a beachfront restaurant. To reach

Damme, you can rent a bike or take a 20-minute bus ride for around €3. The Belgian Coast is accessible by train from Bruges, with a journey time of 15-30 minutes depending on the town, and tickets cost approximately €6 each way. Spring and summer are the best times to visit, as the weather is ideal for outdoor activities.

From Brussels, you can explore the university city of **Leuven** and the historic battlefield of **Waterloo**. Leuven is a vibrant city with a youthful energy, thanks to its large student population. You can visit the stunning Gothic Town Hall, wander through the tranquil Groot Begijnhof (a UNESCO-listed beguinage), or sample local beers at the Stella Artois brewery. Waterloo, on the other hand, is a must-visit for history enthusiasts. The site of Napoleon's final defeat in 1815, Waterloo offers a fascinating glimpse into the past with attractions like the Lion's Mound, the Panorama of the Battle, and the Wellington Museum. Leuven is just a 25-minute train ride from Brussels, with tickets costing around €6 each way. Waterloo is accessible by train in 20 minutes, followed by a short bus ride to the battlefield, with combined transportation costs of approximately €10. Leuven is lovely year-round, while Waterloo is best visited in spring or summer when the weather is pleasant for exploring the open-air battlefield.

From Antwerp, a trip to **Mechelen** and the **Port of Antwerp** offers a mix of history and modern industry. Mechelen is a charming city with a rich history, featuring attractions like St. Rumbold's Cathedral, the Palace of Margaret of Austria, and the Kazerne Dossin Holocaust Museum. The Port of Antwerp, one of the largest in Europe, offers a fascinating look at the city's maritime heritage. You can take a guided boat tour to see the bustling docks and learn about the port's role in global trade. Mechelen is just a 20-minute train ride from Antwerp, with tickets costing around €5 each way. To visit the Port of Antwerp, you can take a tram or bus from the city center, with fares starting at €3. Mechelen is a year-round destination, while the port is best explored in spring or summer when boat tours are in full operation.

From Ghent, the picturesque town of **Oudenaarde** and the scenic **Lys Valley** are perfect for a day trip. Oudenaarde is known for its tapestry heritage and the stunning Town Hall, which houses the Museum of Oudenaarde and the Flemish Ardennes. The Lys Valley, often called the "Golden River," is a haven for nature lovers and artists, with its peaceful waterways, charming villages, and lush landscapes. You can enjoy a boat ride, visit local art galleries, or simply relax by the river. Oudenaarde is a 30-minute train ride from Ghent, with tickets costing around €7 each way. The Lys Valley can be explored by bike or car, with rental options available in Ghent. Spring and autumn are the best times to visit, as the valley is particularly beautiful when the flowers are in bloom or the leaves are changing color.

Transportation Options for Day Trips

Belgium's transportation system is highly efficient, making it easy to plan day trips from any major city. Trains are the most convenient option, with frequent services connecting cities and towns across the country. The **SNCB** website and app are excellent resources for checking schedules and booking tickets. Regional trains are affordable, with fares typically ranging from €5 to €15 for one-way trips. For international destinations like Amsterdam or Paris, high-speed trains such as Thalys and Eurostar are available, though it's best to book these tickets in advance for the lowest prices.

Buses are another option, particularly for smaller towns or destinations not directly served by trains. Companies like **De Lijn** and **TEC** operate extensive networks, with fares starting at €3 for short journeys. Tickets can be purchased online, at stations, or via mobile apps. If you prefer more flexibility, renting a car is a great choice, especially for exploring rural areas like the Lys Valley or the Ardennes. Major car rental companies like **Hertz** and **Europcar** have offices in cities and airports, with daily rates starting at around €40. Be sure to check parking options and road tolls when planning your trip.

Navigating Belgium's transportation systems is straightforward, but it's always a good idea to plan your route in advance. Apps like **Google Maps** and **Citymapper** are invaluable for finding the best connections, while the **SNCB app** provides real-time updates on train services. For international trips, check visa requirements and ensure you have all necessary travel documents.

Seasonal Considerations

The time of year can greatly influence your day trip experience, so it's important to plan accordingly. Spring is one of the best seasons for day trips, as the weather is mild and the countryside is in full bloom. This is the perfect time to visit destinations like Damme or the Lys Valley, where the natural beauty is at its peak. Many outdoor attractions, such as gardens and parks, are at their most beautiful during this season.

Summer is ideal for beach outings and outdoor adventures. Head to the Belgian Coast to enjoy the sandy beaches of Knokke-Heist or explore the hiking trails and rivers of the Ardennes. Keep in mind that summer is also peak tourist season, so popular destinations may be crowded. Booking tickets and accommodations in advance is highly recommended.

Autumn offers a quieter and more atmospheric experience, with fewer crowds and stunning fall foliage. This is a great time to visit historic cities like Oudenaarde or Leuven, as the cooler weather is perfect for walking tours and outdoor exploration. Many towns also host harvest festivals and seasonal markets during this time.

Winter brings a magical charm to Belgium and its neighboring countries, with festive Christmas markets and cozy indoor attractions. Bruges, Ghent, and Brussels are particularly enchanting during the holiday season, with twinkling lights, ice skating rinks, and mulled wine stalls. If you're venturing further afield, consider a trip to Cologne or Aachen in Germany, both of which are famous for their Christmas markets.

CHAPTER 13
LANGUAGE AND COMMUNICATION

Belgium is a multilingual country with a rich cultural heritage, and understanding its language landscape can greatly enhance your travel experience. While navigating a country with multiple official languages may seem daunting, this guide will help you feel confident and prepared to communicate effectively during your trip. From learning basic phrases to understanding cultural norms, here's everything you need to know about language and communication in Belgium.

Language Overview

Belgium has three official languages: **Dutch**, **French**, and **German**, with usage varying by region.

- **Dutch (Flemish)**: Spoken in **Flanders**, the northern part of Belgium, Dutch is the most widely spoken language in the country.
- **French**: Predominantly spoken in **Wallonia**, the southern region, and in **Brussels**, where French is more commonly used despite the city being officially bilingual.

- **German**: Spoken by a small community in the eastern part of Belgium near the German border.

English is widely understood, especially in tourist areas, major cities, and among younger generations. In cities like Brussels, Antwerp, and Bruges, you'll find that many locals, particularly those working in hotels, restaurants, and attractions, are fluent in English. However, in smaller towns or rural areas, English proficiency may be more limited, so learning a few basic phrases in Dutch or French can go a long way in building goodwill and making your interactions smoother.

Common Phrases and Greetings

Using a few simple phrases in the local language can make a big difference in your interactions with locals. Here are some essential phrases in both **Dutch** and **French** to help you navigate common situations:

Greetings and Politeness

- Hello:
    - Dutch: *Hallo / Goedendag*
    - French: *Bonjour*
- Goodbye:
    - Dutch: *Tot ziens*
    - French: *Au revoir*

- Please:
  - Dutch: *Alstublieft*
  - French: *S'il vous plaît*
- Thank you:
  - Dutch: *Dank u wel*
  - French: *Merci*
- You're welcome:
  - Dutch: *Graag gedaan*
  - French: *De rien*
- Excuse me / Sorry:
  - Dutch: *Excuseer / Sorry*
  - French: *Excusez-moi / Pardon*

Asking for Help

- Do you speak English?
  - Dutch: *Spreekt u Engels?*
  - French: *Parlez-vous anglais?*
- I don't understand:
  - Dutch: *Ik begrijp het niet*
  - French: *Je ne comprends pas*
- Where is…?
  - Dutch: *Waar is…?*
  - French: *Où est…?*

Numbers (1-10)

- Dutch: Eén, Twee, Drie, Vier, Vijf, Zes, Zeven, Acht, Negen, Tien

- French: Un, Deux, Trois, Quatre, Cinq, Six, Sept, Huit, Neuf, Dix

Using English in Belgium

English is widely spoken in Belgium, particularly in tourist-centric establishments like hotels, restaurants, and museums. In major cities such as Brussels, Antwerp, and Bruges, you'll rarely encounter significant language barriers. However, in smaller towns or rural areas, English proficiency may be less common, so it's helpful to have a backup plan.

When interacting with locals who may not speak English fluently, speak slowly and clearly, and avoid using slang or idiomatic expressions. Gestures and body language can also help convey your message. If you're struggling to communicate, a translation app can be a lifesaver.

Translation Apps and Tools

Translation apps are incredibly useful for navigating language barriers in Belgium. Here are some recommended tools:

- **Google Translate**: Offers text, voice, and camera translation for both Dutch and French. The offline mode is particularly helpful for translating signs or menus when you don't have internet access.

- **iTranslate**: A user-friendly app with voice-to-voice translation and offline capabilities.
- **SayHi**: Great for real-time voice translation, making it easy to have conversations in Dutch or French.
- **Reverso Context**: Ideal for translating phrases and understanding their context in real-life situations.

Before your trip, download these apps and save key phrases for offline use to ensure you're prepared for any situation.

Communication Etiquette

Belgians value politeness and respect in communication, so it's important to be mindful of cultural norms. Always greet people with a friendly "Bonjour" or "Goedendag" before starting a conversation, and use "please" (*s'il vous plaît* or *alstublieft*) and "thank you" (*merci* or *dank u wel*) frequently.

In formal settings, address people using their title and last name until invited to use their first name. Personal space is respected, so avoid standing too close during conversations. Handshakes are the standard greeting in professional or formal situations, while close friends may exchange three kisses on the cheek (alternating sides), though this varies by region.

Body Language and Non-Verbal Communication

Non-verbal communication is subtle in Belgium, and it's important to be aware of certain customs:

- Avoid pointing at people, as it can be considered rude.
- Maintain eye contact during conversations, as it conveys attentiveness and respect.
- Avoid overly expressive gestures or loud behavior, as Belgians tend to value discretion and calmness.

Signs and Menus

In tourist areas, you'll often find signs and menus available in English, especially in cities like Brussels, Bruges, and Antwerp. However, in smaller towns or local establishments, this may not always be the case. If you encounter a menu or sign in Dutch or French, use a translation app to decipher it or look for familiar words. Learning a few food-related phrases, such as "chicken" (*kip* in Dutch, *poulet* in French) or "vegetarian" (*vegetarisch* in Dutch, *végétarien* in French), can also be helpful.

CHAPTER 14
ITINERARIES FOR EVERY TRAVELER

Itineraries for Solo Travelers

Belgium is a fantastic destination for solo travelers, offering a mix of vibrant cities, charming towns, and cultural experiences that are easy to explore on your own. With its compact size, excellent public transportation, and friendly locals, Belgium makes solo travel both exciting and stress-free. Whether you're planning a short getaway, a week-long adventure, or a two-week immersive journey, these itineraries are designed to help you make the most of your time while enjoying the freedom and flexibility of solo travel.

3-Day Itinerary: Highlights of Belgium

This itinerary is perfect for solo travelers with limited time, focusing on must-see attractions and activities that are easy to navigate.

Day 1: Brussels – The Heart of Belgium

Start your trip in Brussels, the capital of Belgium and the European Union. Begin your day at the **Grand Place**, a UNESCO World Heritage Site and one of the most beautiful squares in Europe. Take your time exploring the surrounding streets, filled with chocolate shops, cafes, and boutiques.

Visit the **Atomium**, an iconic structure offering panoramic views of the city, and explore the nearby **Mini-Europe**, a miniature park featuring famous European landmarks. For lunch, try **Chez Léon**, a casual spot known for its mussels and fries.

In the afternoon, visit the **Magritte Museum**, dedicated to the works of the surrealist artist René Magritte. End your day with dinner at **Comme Chez Soi**, a Michelin-starred restaurant offering a fine dining experience. Stay overnight at **Meininger Hotel Brussels City Center**, a budget-friendly option with a social atmosphere perfect for meeting other travelers.

Day 2: Bruges – A Fairytale City

Take a morning train to Bruges, a city that feels like stepping into a storybook. Start with a canal boat tour to see the city from the water, then visit the **Basilica of the Holy Blood** and the **Belfry of Bruges** for stunning views.

For lunch, try **De Halve Maan Brewery**, where you can enjoy hearty Belgian dishes and sample their beer. Spend the afternoon wandering through the **Begijnhof**, a peaceful courtyard surrounded by whitewashed houses, or visit the **Groeningemuseum** to admire Flemish art.

In the evening, enjoy a casual dinner at **The Olive Tree**, a cozy Mediterranean restaurant. Stay overnight at **St. Christopher's Inn Hostel**, a great place to meet fellow travelers.

Day 3: Ghent – A Blend of History and Modernity

On your final day, take a short train ride to Ghent, a lively city with a mix of history and modern charm. Visit **Gravensteen Castle**, a medieval fortress with stunning views from the top. Stroll along the **Graslei and Korenlei**, two picturesque quays lined with historic buildings, and enjoy a coffee at one of the riverside cafes.

For lunch, try **Pakhuis**, a stylish brasserie housed in a former warehouse. In the afternoon, explore the **St. Bavo's Cathedral**, home to the famous Ghent Altarpiece, or take a walk through **Citadel Park**. Return to Brussels in the evening or stay overnight in Ghent.

7-Day Itinerary: A Week of Exploration

This week-long itinerary builds on the 3-day plan, adding more destinations and opportunities for cultural immersion.

Day 1-3: Brussels, Bruges, and Ghent

Follow the 3-day itinerary, but add a visit to the **Royal Palace of Brussels** (if open) and a chocolate-making workshop in Bruges for a sweet and interactive experience.

Day 4: Antwerp – Art and Fashion

Travel to Antwerp, a city known for its fashion, art, and diamonds. Visit the **Cathedral of Our Lady**, home to works by Rubens, and explore the **Museum aan de Stroom (MAS)**, which offers panoramic views from its rooftop terrace.

For lunch, try **The Jane**, a Michelin-starred restaurant with a stunning interior. Spend the afternoon shopping for diamonds or exploring the **ModeMuseum**, dedicated to Antwerp's fashion heritage. Stay overnight at **Antwerp Central Youth Hostel**, a budget-friendly option with a central location.

Day 5: Leuven – A Charming University City

Take a day trip to Leuven, a vibrant university city with a romantic vibe. Visit the **Groot Begijnhof**, a UNESCO-listed beguinage, and the **M-Museum**, which features contemporary and classical art. Enjoy lunch at **Zarza**, a stylish restaurant with a creative menu. Spend the afternoon exploring the city's botanical garden or sampling local beers at the **Stella Artois Brewery**.

Day 6: Belgian Coast – Relaxation by the Sea

Head to the Belgian Coast for a day of relaxation. Visit Knokke-Heist, a chic seaside town with sandy beaches and upscale boutiques. Rent bikes and explore the **Zwin Nature Park**, a peaceful reserve perfect for birdwatching. Enjoy fresh seafood at **Brasserie Rubens** before returning to your hotel.

Day 7: Pairi Daiza – A World-Class Zoo

Spend your final day at **Pairi Daiza**, a world-class zoo and botanical garden located about an hour from Brussels. It's home to pandas, elephants, and other exotic animals, as well as themed areas like an African savanna and a Chinese garden.

14-Day Itinerary: Immersive Belgian Adventure

This two-week itinerary offers a comprehensive and varied plan, blending sightseeing, relaxation, and unique experiences.

Days 1-7: Follow the 7-Day Itinerary

Start with the 7-day plan, adding a visit to the **Royal Palace of Brussels** (if open) and a chocolate-making workshop in Bruges for a sweet and interactive experience.

Days 8-9: Ardennes – Nature and Adventure

Travel to the Ardennes, a region of rolling hills, dense forests, and charming villages. Stay in Durbuy, often called the "smallest city in the world." Go hiking, kayaking on the Ourthe River, or explore the **Caves of Han**. Stay at **Le Sanglier des Ardennes**, a luxurious hotel with a spa and gourmet restaurant.

Days 10-11: Mechelen and Pairi Daiza

Visit Mechelen, a charming city with a rich history. Climb the **St. Rumbold's Tower** for panoramic views, and enjoy lunch at **De Vleeshalle**, a trendy food market. Spend the next day at **Pairi Daiza**, a world-class zoo and botanical garden that's perfect for couples who love animals and nature.

Days 12-13: Spa – Relaxation and Luxury

Indulge in a spa retreat in the town of Spa, the birthplace of wellness tourism. Relax in the thermal baths, enjoy a couples' massage, and explore the surrounding countryside. Stay at **Hotel Manoir de Lébioles**, a romantic château with luxurious amenities.

Day 14: Brussels – A Sweet Farewell

End your trip with a leisurely day in Brussels. Visit the **Magritte Museum**, enjoy a final Belgian waffle at **Maison Dandoy**, and take a romantic walk through the **Parc de Bruxelles** before heading home.

Belgium offers endless opportunities for solo travelers, from its fairytale cities to its tranquil countryside. With these tailored itineraries, you'll have all the tools you need to create a trip that's enjoyable, stress-free, and filled with unforgettable memories.

Itineraries for Couples

Belgium is a dream destination for couples, offering a blend of romantic cities, charming villages, and intimate experiences. Whether you're planning a short romantic escape, a week-long adventure, or a two-week journey, Belgium has everything you need to create unforgettable memories with your partner. From cozy dining spots to scenic day trips and luxurious experiences, these itineraries are designed to help you connect, relax, and explore together.

3-Day Romantic Getaway

This itinerary is perfect for couples looking for a short but magical escape, focusing on iconic landmarks, intimate activities, and cozy dining experiences.

Day 1: Brussels – A Romantic Start

Begin your trip in Brussels, where you can explore the **Grand Place**, one of the most beautiful squares in Europe. Stroll hand-in-hand through the cobblestone streets, admiring the ornate guildhalls and the romantic atmosphere. Visit the **Atomium**, where you can enjoy panoramic views of the city from the top sphere.

For lunch, head to **La Roue d'Or**, a charming restaurant near the Grand Place that serves traditional Belgian cuisine in an intimate setting. In the afternoon, visit the **Royal Greenhouses of Laeken** (if in season) or take a leisurely walk through the **Mont des Arts Garden**, a peaceful spot with stunning views of the city.

End your day with a romantic dinner at **Comme Chez Soi**, a Michelin-starred restaurant known for its exquisite cuisine and elegant ambiance. Stay overnight at **Hotel Amigo**, a luxurious hotel just steps from the Grand Place, offering stylish rooms and impeccable service.

Day 2: Bruges – A Fairytale Escape

Take a morning train to Bruges, often called the "Venice of the North." Start your day with a canal boat tour, gliding through the city's picturesque waterways. Visit the **Basilica of the Holy Blood** and climb the **Belfry of Bruges** for breathtaking views of the city.

For lunch, try **De Halve Maan Brewery**, where you can enjoy hearty Belgian dishes and sample their famous beer. Spend the afternoon wandering through the **Begijnhof**, a tranquil courtyard surrounded by whitewashed houses, or visit the **Groeningemuseum** to admire Flemish art.

In the evening, enjoy a candlelit dinner at **Den Gouden Harynck**, a romantic restaurant with a cozy atmosphere and refined cuisine. Stay overnight at **Hotel de Orangerie**, a boutique hotel overlooking the canal, known for its elegant décor and intimate charm.

Day 3: Ghent – A Blend of History and Romance

On your final day, take a short train ride to Ghent, a lively city with a mix of history and modern charm. Visit **Gravensteen Castle**, a medieval fortress with stunning views from the top. Stroll along the **Graslei and Korenlei**, two picturesque quays lined with historic buildings, and enjoy a coffee at one of the riverside cafés.

For lunch, try **Pakhuis**, a stylish brasserie housed in a former warehouse. In the afternoon, explore the **St. Bavo's Cathedral**, home to the famous Ghent Altarpiece, or take a romantic walk through **Citadel Park**.

Return to Brussels in the evening, or extend your stay in Ghent for one more night of romance.

7-Day Romantic Adventure

This week-long itinerary builds on the 3-day plan, adding more in-depth experiences, day trips, and leisure days to create a perfect balance of exploration and relaxation.

Day 1-3: Brussels and Bruges

Follow the 3-day itinerary for Brussels and Bruges, but add a visit to **Mini-Europe** in Brussels, where you can explore miniature versions of Europe's landmarks, and the **Frietmuseum** in Bruges, a quirky museum dedicated to Belgian fries.

Day 4: Antwerp – Art and Elegance

Travel to Antwerp, a city known for its fashion, art, and diamonds. Visit the **Cathedral of Our Lady**, home to works by Rubens, and explore the **Museum aan de Stroom (MAS)**, which offers panoramic views from its rooftop terrace.

For lunch, try **The Jane**, a Michelin-starred restaurant with a stunning interior. Spend the afternoon shopping for diamonds or exploring the **ModeMuseum**, dedicated to Antwerp's fashion heritage. End your day with a romantic dinner at **Het Gebaar**, a cozy restaurant with a beautiful garden. Stay overnight at **Hotel Julien**, a chic boutique hotel in the heart of the city.

Day 5: Leuven – A Charming Day Trip

Take a day trip to Leuven, a vibrant university city with a romantic vibe. Visit the **Groot Begijnhof**, a UNESCO-listed beguinage, and the **M-Museum**, which features contemporary and classical art. Enjoy lunch at **Zarza**, a stylish restaurant with a creative menu. Spend the afternoon exploring the city's botanical garden or sampling local beers at the **Stella Artois Brewery**.

Day 6: Belgian Coast – Relaxation by the Sea

Head to the Belgian Coast for a day of relaxation. Visit Knokke-Heist, a chic seaside town with sandy beaches and upscale boutiques. Rent bikes and explore the **Zwin Nature Park**, a peaceful reserve perfect for birdwatching. Enjoy fresh seafood at **Brasserie Rubens** before returning to your hotel.

Day 7: Ghent – A Romantic Finale

Wrap up your trip in Ghent, following the 3-day itinerary suggestions. Add a visit to the **Design Museum** or take a sunset boat tour for a magical end to your journey.

14-Day Romantic Escape

This two-week itinerary offers a comprehensive and varied plan, blending sightseeing, relaxation, and unique romantic activities to create the ultimate couples' getaway.

Days 1-7: Follow the 7-Day Itinerary

Start with the 7-day plan, adding a visit to the **Royal Palace of Brussels** (if open) and a chocolate-making workshop in Bruges for a sweet and interactive experience.

Days 8-9: Ardennes – Nature and Adventure

Travel to the Ardennes, a region of rolling hills, dense forests, and charming villages. Stay in Durbuy, often called the "smallest city in the world." Go hiking, kayaking on the Ourthe River, or explore the **Caves of Han**. Stay at **Le Sanglier des Ardennes**, a luxurious hotel with a spa and gourmet restaurant.

Days 10-11: Mechelen and Pairi Daiza

Visit Mechelen, a charming city with a rich history. Climb the **St. Rumbold's Tower** for panoramic views, and enjoy lunch at **De Vleeshalle**, a trendy food market. Spend the next day at **Pairi Daiza**, a world-class zoo and botanical garden that's perfect for couples who love animals and nature.

Days 12-13: Spa – Relaxation and Luxury

Indulge in a spa retreat in the town of Spa, the birthplace of wellness tourism. Relax in the thermal baths, enjoy a couples' massage, and explore the surrounding countryside.

Stay at **Hotel Manoir de Lébioles**, a romantic château with luxurious amenities.

Day 14: Brussels – A Sweet Farewell

End your trip with a leisurely day in Brussels. Visit the **Magritte Museum**, enjoy a final Belgian waffle at **Maison Dandoy**, and take a romantic walk through the **Parc de Bruxelles** before heading home.

Itineraries for Families

Belgium is a fantastic destination for families, offering a mix of fun, educational, and relaxing activities that cater to both children and parents. From interactive museums and zoos to charming towns and outdoor adventures, there's something for everyone. Whether you're planning a short getaway or a two-week vacation, these tailored itineraries will help you make the most of your time in Belgium while keeping the whole family happy and engaged.

3-Day Family Itinerary: A Short and Sweet Adventure

This itinerary is perfect for families with young children or those looking for a quick, manageable trip. It focuses on activities that are fun, interactive, and easy to navigate.

Day 1: Brussels – Interactive Fun and Chocolate Treats

Start your trip in Brussels, where you can visit the **Belgian Comic Strip Center**, a colorful museum dedicated to beloved characters like Tintin and the Smurfs. Kids will love the interactive exhibits, while parents can appreciate the artistry of Belgian comics. Afterward, head to the **Royal Greenhouses of Laeken** (open seasonally in spring) or the **Parc du Cinquantenaire**, where children can run around and enjoy the open space.

For lunch, try **Chez Léon**, a family-friendly restaurant near the Grand Place that serves Belgian classics like mussels and fries. In the afternoon, treat the kids to a chocolate-making workshop at **Choco-Story Brussels**, where they can learn about Belgium's famous chocolate and create their own sweet treats.

Day 2: Antwerp – Animals and Hands-On Learning

Take a short train ride to Antwerp, home to the **Antwerp Zoo**, one of the oldest and most beautiful zoos in Europe. Located right next to the train station, it's easy to access and features a wide variety of animals, including elephants, lions, and penguins. After lunch at the zoo's café, visit the **MAS Museum**, which has family-friendly exhibits and stunning views from its rooftop terrace.

For dinner, head to **Otto's Burger**, a casual spot with kid-approved meals.

Day 3: Bruges – Fairy Tales and Swans

End your trip in Bruges, a magical city that feels like stepping into a storybook. Take a family-friendly canal boat tour to see the city from the water, then visit the **Historium Bruges**, an interactive museum that brings medieval Bruges to life. Kids will enjoy the virtual reality experience, while parents can appreciate the historical insights.

For lunch, try **De Halve Maan Brewery**, which has a kid-friendly menu and a lovely courtyard. Spend the afternoon at **Minnewater Park**, where children can feed the swans and parents can relax in the peaceful surroundings.

Tips for Traveling with Kids:

- Use Belgium's efficient train system to minimize travel stress.
- Pack snacks, water, and small toys to keep kids entertained during transit.
- Plan for rest breaks at parks or cafés to recharge.

7-Day Family Itinerary: A Week of Fun and Exploration

This week-long itinerary balances active days with relaxed ones, giving families time to explore Belgium's highlights while ensuring everyone stays energized.

Day 1-2: Brussels

Spend the first two days exploring Brussels. In addition to the activities from the 3-day itinerary, visit **Mini-Europe**, a miniature park featuring replicas of famous European landmarks. It's both fun and educational for kids. Don't miss the **Atomium**, where you can take an elevator to the top for panoramic views.

Day 3: Ghent

Take a day trip to Ghent, a lively city with a mix of history and modern charm. Visit **Gravensteen Castle**, a medieval fortress with exhibits and stunning views from the top. Afterward, explore the **STAM Museum**, which has interactive displays about the city's history.

Day 4: Pairi Daiza

Spend the day at **Pairi Daiza**, a world-class zoo and botanical garden located about an hour from Brussels. It's home to pandas, elephants, and other exotic animals, as well as themed areas like an African savanna and a Chinese garden.

Day 5: Bruges

Follow the Bruges itinerary from the 3-day plan, but add a visit to the **Frietmuseum**, a quirky museum dedicated to Belgian fries.

Day 6: Belgian Coast

Take a day trip to the Belgian Coast, where you can relax on the sandy beaches of Knokke-Heist or explore the dunes at De Haan. Rent bikes or take a ride on the **Coastal Tram**, which connects the seaside towns.

Day 7: Antwerp

Wrap up your trip in Antwerp, adding a visit to the **Chocolate Nation Museum**, where kids can learn about the history of Belgian chocolate and enjoy tastings.

Tips for Traveling with Kids:

- Alternate busy sightseeing days with slower-paced ones to avoid burnout.
- Book tickets for popular attractions in advance to save time.
- Choose accommodations with family-friendly amenities, such as extra beds or kitchenettes.

14-Day Family Itinerary: A Comprehensive Belgian Adventure

This two-week itinerary combines major attractions, outdoor adventures, and cultural experiences, ensuring a memorable trip for the whole family.

Days 1-3: Brussels

Follow the Brussels itinerary from the 7-day plan, but add a visit to the **Train World Museum**, where kids can explore historic locomotives.

Days 4-5: Ardennes

Head to the Ardennes for outdoor adventures. Stay in Durbuy, a charming town surrounded by nature. Go kayaking on the Ourthe River, explore the **Caves of Han**, or visit the **Wildlife Park**.

Days 6-7: Ghent and Oudenaarde

Spend a day in Ghent, then take a day trip to Oudenaarde in the Flemish Ardennes. Visit the **MOU Museum** and enjoy a family bike ride through the scenic countryside.

Days 8-9: Bruges and Damme

Follow the Bruges itinerary from the 7-day plan, but add a bike ride to Damme, a picturesque village just outside Bruges.

Days 10-11: Antwerp and Mechelen

Explore Antwerp, then take a day trip to Mechelen. Visit **Technopolis**, a hands-on science museum that's perfect for kids, and the **Toy Museum**, which features an impressive collection of toys from around the world.

Days 12-13: Belgian Coast and Pairi Daiza

Spend a day at the coast, then revisit Pairi Daiza for a more relaxed experience.

Day 14: Leuven

End your trip in Leuven, where you can explore the **M Museum** and enjoy a leisurely walk through the **Botanical Garden**.

CONCLUSION

Belgium is a country that truly has it all. From the cobblestone streets of Bruges to the vibrant energy of Brussels, the artistic flair of Antwerp, and the historic charm of Ghent, every corner of Belgium offers something unique and unforgettable. Whether you're marveling at the intricate beauty of the Grand Place, cruising along picturesque canals, savoring world-class chocolate and beer, or exploring the rolling hills of the Ardennes, Belgium is a destination that captivates your heart and leaves you wanting more.

What makes Belgium so special is its diversity. It's a place where history and modernity blend seamlessly, where you can admire medieval castles in the morning and enjoy cutting-edge art galleries in the afternoon. It's a country that invites you to slow down and savor life, whether you're indulging in a leisurely meal of mussels and fries, wandering through a peaceful beguinage, or simply sitting at a café, watching the world go by. And let's not forget the warmth of the Belgian people, who welcome you with open arms and make you feel at home no matter where you go.

Now that you've explored this guide, you have everything you need to start planning your Belgian adventure. From practical tips to tailored itineraries, this guide is your companion to discovering the best of Belgium. Whether you're traveling solo, as a couple, with family, or in a group,

Belgium offers endless opportunities to create memories that will last a lifetime.

So why wait? The cobblestone streets, the aroma of freshly baked waffles, the glittering canals, and the vibrant festivals are calling your name. It's time to turn your dream trip into a reality. Pack your bags, book your tickets, and get ready to immerse yourself in the magic of Belgium.

As you embark on this journey, know that Belgium will surprise and delight you at every turn. It's a place where every moment feels special, where every experience is meaningful, and where every memory is worth cherishing. Whether it's your first visit or your fifth, Belgium has a way of staying with you long after you've left.

So go ahead—explore, indulge, and fall in love with Belgium. The adventure of a lifetime is waiting for you, and it's going to be unforgettable. Safe travels, and enjoy every moment of your Belgian journey!

Printed in Dunstable, United Kingdom